I0781770

HOW TO ROMANCE YOUR HUSBAND

A step-by-step guide on how to communicate, express love, build intimacy, overcome challenges, and create lasting romance with your spouse and make him adore, love, and want you

Emmanuel J Louis

TABLE OF CONTENTS

Introduction

Welcome to "How to Romance Your Husband," a comprehensive guide designed to help you rekindle and sustain the spark in your marriage. Whether you're newlyweds or have been together for decades, this book offers practical advice, heartfelt insights, and actionable strategies to deepen your connection and bring more joy into your relationship.

The Importance of Romance in Marriage

In the hustle and bustle of everyday life, it's easy for romance to take a back seat. Responsibilities such as work, children, household chores, and social obligations can overshadow the intimate moments that initially brought you and your husband together. Yet, maintaining a sense of romance is crucial for a thriving marriage. Romance fosters emotional intimacy, strengthens your bond, and keeps the relationship dynamic and fulfilling.

Dispelling Myths About Romance

Romance is often misunderstood as merely grand gestures or special occasions. While those moments can be significant, true romance is found in the everyday acts of love and thoughtfulness. It's in the small gestures that show your husband he is cherished and valued. This book aims to redefine romance, making it accessible and sustainable in your daily life.

Why This Book?

We will look at several facets of romance in this book and how your marriage might benefit from them. In this book, you will learn and understand various topics and aspects such as:

Recognizing Your Spouse's Love Language: To make sure your husband feels loved and valued in the ways that matter most to him, learn to identify and speak his love language.

Effective Communication:

To strengthen your emotional bond, learn how to promote sincere, transparent, and honest communication.

Developing Intimacy:

Look for methods to improve closeness and passion in your relationship by developing both physical and emotional intimacy.

Supporting One Another:

Recognize the value of mutual assistance and learn how to be a dependable, devoted partner in the face of adversity.

Balancing Responsibilities:

Find strategies for balancing work, family, and romance to maintain a harmonious and loving household.

Coping with Stress:

Learn methods to manage stress and fatigue without letting them erode your relationship.

Growing Together:

Engage in shared activities and mutual growth, strengthening your bond and ensuring you evolve together as a couple.

Planning a Future Together:

Create a shared vision for your future, setting goals and making plans that reflect your shared values and aspirations.

This book is designed to be both inspirational and practical. Each chapter includes actionable tips and exercises to help you apply the concepts to your marriage. Take your time with each section, reflecting on how the ideas can be integrated into your relationship.

A Journey Worth Taking

Romancing your husband is a journey that requires intention, effort, and love. It's about creating a partnership where both of you feel valued, understood, and cherished. As you embark on this journey, remember that the rewards are immense: a deeper connection, a stronger bond, and a more joyful and fulfilling marriage.

Thank you for choosing "How to Romance Your Husband." I hope this book becomes a valuable resource and inspiration as you work to enhance your relationship and build a lifetime of love and romance. Here's to a beautiful journey ahead!

Chapter 1

Understanding Your Husband

What Romance Means to Men

Understanding what romance means to men is a crucial starting point for anyone looking to deepen their romantic relationship. Romance can be perceived differently by each individual, but there are some common themes and preferences that tend to resonate with many men.

Understanding Individual Preferences

Romance is not a one-size-fits-all concept. Each man has unique tastes, preferences, and experiences that shape his understanding of romance. Some men may appreciate grand gestures, while others might value simple, everyday acts of love. It's essential to know your husband's specific preferences and tailor your romantic efforts to what makes him feel loved and appreciated.

Common Romantic Themes

Feeling Appreciated and Valued: Many men associate romance with feeling respected, admired, and appreciated.

Simple acknowledgments of his efforts and expressions of gratitude can have a significant romantic impact.

Physical Touch and Affection: Physical expressions of love, such as hugs, kisses, and cuddling, are important aspects of romance for many men. These gestures can reinforce emotional bonds and create a sense of closeness.

Shared Activities and Interests: Engaging in activities that he enjoys or sharing a common hobby can be a romantic gesture. Whether it's watching his favorite sports team, playing a game together, or embarking on an adventure, shared experiences can strengthen your bond.

Quality Time: Spending undistracted time together is crucial. This might include talking, going for walks, or simply enjoying each other's company without the interference of work or technology.

Thoughtful Surprises: Small, thoughtful surprises can make a big difference. This could be anything from a favorite meal, a handwritten note, or a planned date night. These gestures show that you are thinking of him and that you value your relationship.

Communication is Key

Understanding what romance means to your husband requires open and honest communication. Discussing what each of you finds romantic and what makes you feel loved can lead to a more fulfilling relationship. Ask questions, share your thoughts, and be willing to listen. This dialogue can help you both understand each other's needs and desires better.

Practical Tips

Pay Attention to His Reactions: Notice how he responds to different romantic gestures. This can give you clues about what he values most.

Be Genuine: Authenticity matters. Romantic gestures should come from a place of genuine love and care, not out of obligation.

Be Patient and Observant: Sometimes, it might take a while to understand what your husband finds romantic. Be patient and keep observing his responses to different actions and gestures.

Balance Efforts: Romance should be a two-way street. While you're making efforts to romance your husband, encourage him to express his love and romance in his way as well.

By understanding and embracing what romance means to your husband, you can create a more loving, fulfilling, and connected relationship. This understanding forms the foundation for the rest of the romantic efforts you will make in your marriage.

The Psychology of Male Romance

Understanding the psychology of male romance involves delving into the mental and emotional processes that shape how men perceive and express romantic feelings. This understanding can help you connect with your husband on a deeper level, fostering a more fulfilling and harmonious relationship.

Biological and Evolutionary Factors

Evolutionary Psychology: From an evolutionary standpoint, men and women have developed different strategies for attracting and retaining mates. Men may be more inclined towards actions that demonstrate their ability to provide and protect. Understanding this can help explain why some men might equate romantic gestures with practical demonstrations of care and support.

Hormonal Influences: Testosterone, the primary male sex hormone, plays a significant role in behavior and emotional responses. While higher levels of testosterone are often linked to competitiveness and aggression, they are also associated with the drive to pursue and maintain romantic relationships.

Social and Cultural Conditioning

Cultural Norms and Expectations: Societal norms heavily influence how men perceive and express romance. Many cultures promote the idea that men should be strong, stoic, and less emotionally expressive. These norms can sometimes hinder men from fully engaging in romantic behaviors that they might actually desire.

Media and Pop Culture: Movies, TV shows, and books often portray certain stereotypes about male romance, such as the notion that men are less interested in emotional intimacy. These portrayals can shape men's understanding of romance and influence their behavior in relationships.

Emotional and Psychological Needs

Need for Validation and Appreciation: Men, like women, have a strong need to feel valued and appreciated in their relationships. Acts of recognition, verbal affirmations, and showing gratitude can significantly impact a man's sense of self-worth and his romantic engagement.

Desire for Emotional Security: Emotional security is crucial for everyone. For men, feeling secure in a relationship often means knowing that they are respected and their efforts are recognized. This security can foster a deeper emotional connection and enhance romantic expression.

Affection and Intimacy: Contrary to some stereotypes, men often crave affection and intimacy. Physical touch, such as holding hands, hugging, and cuddling, can be powerful expressions of love and connection for men. Emotional intimacy, where they feel understood and supported, is equally important.

Communication Styles

Direct Communication: Men often prefer direct communication and may not pick up on subtle hints or indirect messages as easily. Clear and straightforward communication about desires, needs, and feelings can help in fostering romance.

Action-Oriented Expression: Many men express their love and romantic feelings through actions rather than words. This might include fixing things around the house, providing support, or planning activities that they know their partner enjoys.

Overcoming Barriers to Romantic Expression

Fear of Vulnerability: Many men struggle with being vulnerable due to societal expectations and fear of rejection. Creating a safe space where vulnerability is welcomed and respected can help men open up emotionally and engage more deeply in romantic behaviors.

Stress and External Pressures: Work, financial concerns, and other external pressures can impact a man's ability to engage in romance. Understanding and supporting your husband through these challenges can help alleviate stress and create a more conducive environment for romance.

Practical Strategies

Encourage Open Dialogue: Regularly talk about each other's romantic needs and preferences. Encourage your husband to share his feelings and listen without judgment.

Show Appreciation: Regularly express gratitude for his efforts, both big and small. Recognition and appreciation can boost his confidence and willingness to engage in romantic behaviors.

Be Attentive to His Love Language: Understand and respond to his love language, whether it's words of affirmation, acts of service, receiving gifts, quality time, or physical touch. Tailoring your romantic gestures to his love language can make a significant impact.

Encourage His Interests: Show a genuine interest in his pastimes and pursuits. Taking part in or encouraging his hobbies might lead to shared experiences that improve your relationship romantically.

Show Understanding and Patience: It's vital to be patient and tolerant as you both travel through your romantic adventure because romance can change over time.

Understanding His Needs and Desires

A fulfilling romantic relationship hinges on understanding and addressing each other's needs and desires. When you comprehend what your husband truly values and yearns for, you can create a more intimate and supportive connection.

How to understand your husband's needs and desires includes;

Identifying Core Needs

Emotional Support: One of the primary needs for many men is emotional support. This includes feeling understood, validated, and cared for. Emotional support can be demonstrated through active listening, empathy, and being there during tough times.

Respect and Admiration: Men often have a strong need to feel respected and admired by their partners. This can involve acknowledging his strengths, accomplishments, and efforts both in the relationship and in other aspects of his life.

Physical Intimacy: Physical closeness is crucial for many men. This goes beyond sexual intimacy to include gestures like holding hands, hugging, and cuddling. Physical intimacy helps reinforce the emotional bond and fosters a sense of closeness.

Recreational Companionship: Sharing activities and hobbies can be significant for men. Whether it's playing sports, watching movies, or working on projects together, recreational companionship helps create shared experiences and strengthens the relationship.

Autonomy and Independence: While connection is vital, men also need a sense of independence and autonomy. Supporting his need for personal space and time to pursue his interests is important for a balanced and healthy relationship.

Communicating About Needs

Open Dialogue: Encourage open and honest conversations about each other's needs and desires. Create a safe space where he feels comfortable sharing without fear of judgment or criticism.

Ask Specific Questions: Sometimes, general questions like "What do you need?" may not elicit clear responses. Instead, ask specific questions such as, "What can I do to make you feel more appreciated?" or "What activities do you enjoy us doing together?"

Active Listening: Practice active listening when he shares his needs and desires. This involves paying full attention, reflecting on what he says, and asking follow-up questions to ensure you understand his perspective.

Recognizing Unspoken Needs

Body Language and Non-Verbal Cues: Pay attention to his body language and non-verbal cues. Sometimes, men may not verbally express their needs, but their actions, facial expressions, and gestures can provide insights into what they desire.

Observing Patterns: Notice patterns in his behavior and responses to different situations. For instance, if he becomes more affectionate after certain activities or seems withdrawn when stressed, these patterns can help you understand his needs better.

Emotional Reactions: Observe his emotional reactions to various experiences. Positive reactions can indicate what he values, while negative reactions can highlight unmet needs or areas of discomfort.

Meeting His Desires

Personalized Romantic Gestures: Tailor your romantic gestures to his preferences. If he enjoys quality time, plan activities you can do together. If words of affirmation resonate with him, regularly express your appreciation and love.

Supporting His Goals: Show interest and support for his personal and professional goals. Whether celebrating his achievements or providing encouragement during challenging times, your support can be a powerful way to meet his needs.

Creating Balance: Strive to balance your needs with his. Relationships are about mutual give and take, and finding a balance ensures both partners feel fulfilled and valued.

Navigating Challenges

Handling Conflict Constructively: Constructive Conflict Handling: Although disagreements will inevitably arise, how you resolve them will determine how successfully you communicate and accommodate one another's demands. Instead of placing blame, approach confrontations with a resolution and understanding perspective.

Handling Stress: He may find it difficult to communicate and comprehend his demands when under stress. When things are stressful, have patience and offer more assistance. Promote stress-relieving activities that involve relaxation and self-care.

Adjusting to changes: Over time, needs and desires may vary as a result of many life circumstances, including changes in a person's work, health, or family dynamics. Evaluate your relationship on a regular basis and talk about the possible effects of these changes.

Practical Strategies

Routine Check-ins: Schedule regular check-ins to discuss each other's needs and how well they are being met. This proactive approach helps prevent misunderstandings and ensures ongoing connection.

Surprise and Delight: Occasionally, surprise him with something he loves or has mentioned wanting. These spontaneous acts can make him feel cherished and understood.

Continuous Learning: Stay curious and open to learning more about him. People grow and change, and maintaining an attitude of continuous learning about your partner keeps the relationship dynamic and fulfilling.

By understanding and addressing your husband's needs and desires, you create a foundation of trust, respect, and deep connection. This understanding not only enriches your romantic relationship but also fosters a supportive and loving partnership where both of you can thrive.

Breaking Down Stereotypes

Stereotypes about romance, particularly regarding how men experience and express it, can hinder genuine connection and understanding in a relationship. Breaking down these stereotypes is essential to build a deeper, more authentic bond with your husband. This section explores common stereotypes and offers strategies to overcome them.

Common Stereotypes About Male Romance

Men Are Unromantic: A prevalent stereotype is that men are less romantic than women and do not value romance in a relationship. This misconception can lead to neglecting their romantic needs and desires.

Men Only Value Physical Intimacy: Another stereotype is that men are primarily driven by physical desires and are less interested in emotional intimacy. This belief overlooks the complex emotional needs that many men have.

Men Should Be Stoic and Emotionally Reserved: Society often expects men to be stoic and suppress their emotions. This stereotype can prevent men from expressing their feelings and needs openly.

Men Are Not Affected by Small Gestures: There is a notion that men do not appreciate small, thoughtful gestures as much as women do. This underestimates the impact of everyday acts of love and kindness.

Impact of Stereotypes on Relationships

Limited Emotional Expression: Stereotypes can discourage men from expressing their emotions and needs, leading to misunderstandings and a lack of emotional intimacy in the relationship.

Misaligned Expectations: If you adhere to stereotypes, you may have unrealistic or inaccurate expectations of your husband's romantic behaviors and needs, causing frustration and disappointment.

Reduced Effort in Romance: Believing that men do not value romance can result in less effort being put into romantic gestures, thereby diminishing the quality of the relationship.

Strategies to Break Down Stereotypes

Encourage Open Communication

Create a Safe Space: Foster an environment where your husband feels safe to express his feelings and needs without fear of judgment or ridicule.

Ask Direct Questions: Encourage him to share his thoughts on romance by asking direct and open-ended questions. For example, "What makes you feel loved and appreciated?"

Challenge Societal Norms

Educate Yourself: Understand the origins and impacts of stereotypes on men and relationships. Awareness is the first step in challenging and changing these beliefs.

Support Emotional Expression: Encourage your husband to express his emotions and validate his feelings. Show him that being emotionally open is a strength, not a weakness.

Focus on Individual Preferences

Personalize Romantic Gestures: Tailor your romantic efforts to what specifically makes your husband feel loved and appreciated. Avoid generic assumptions based on stereotypes.

Celebrate His Unique Traits: Acknowledge and celebrate the unique ways your husband expresses and experiences romance.

Promote Mutual Understanding

Share Your Own Needs and Desires: Be open about your romantic needs and encourage him to do the same. Mutual understanding fosters a more balanced and fulfilling relationship.

Practice Empathy: Put yourself in his shoes and try to understand his perspective on romance. Empathy can bridge gaps created by stereotypes.

Acknowledge and Appreciate Small Gestures

Recognize Everyday Acts: Show appreciation for the small, everyday things he does to show love and care. These gestures are often overlooked but are significant expressions of romance.

Reciprocate Thoughtfulness: Engage in small acts of kindness and thoughtfulness yourself, creating a reciprocal cycle of appreciation and affection.

Support His Interests and Hobbies

Engage in Shared Activities: Participate in activities and hobbies he enjoys. Shared experiences can enhance your connection and challenge the stereotype that men do not appreciate romantic efforts.

Show Interest in His Passions: Take an active interest in his passions and support his pursuits. This demonstrates that you value his individuality and care about what makes him happy.

Celebrate Emotional Milestones

Acknowledge Emotional Growth: Celebrate moments when he opens up emotionally or shares his feelings. Positive reinforcement can encourage more emotional expression.

Reflect on Progress Together: Regularly reflect on your relationship's growth and the emotional milestones you have achieved together. This reinforces the importance of emotional intimacy.

Practical Tips

Regular Check-ins: Frequent Check-ins: Talk about each other's needs, emotions, and any changes in the dynamics of your relationship during regular check-ins. This supports the upkeep of a strong and developing romantic relationship.

Mindful Language: Pay attention to the words you use. Sayings like "Men don't care about that" should be avoided in favor of focusing on personal preferences and expressions.

Educate and Speak Up: Encourage more accepting and compassionate perspectives on male romance while educating friends and family about the negative impacts of stereotypes.

Stereotypes can be dispelled to foster a more accepting and encouraging atmosphere where couples can express who they are and more successfully fulfill each other's romantic needs. This results in a deeper, more satisfying connection built on respect and understanding for one another.

Chapter 2

Effective Communication

The Importance of Listening

Effective listening is foundational for a strong and healthy relationship. It is not just about hearing the words your partner says, but about understanding and valuing their feelings, thoughts, and needs. In the context of romancing your husband, active and empathetic listening can deepen your emotional connection and foster a more supportive and loving relationship.

What is Active Listening?

Active listening involves fully concentrating, understanding, responding, and remembering what your partner says. It requires more than just passively hearing; it involves engaging with your husband on a deeper level.

Key Elements of Active Listening

Focus and Attention

Eliminate Distractions: Give your full attention to your husband by putting away phones, turning off the TV, and minimizing other distractions.

Maintain Eye Contact: Show that you are engaged and interested by maintaining eye contact. This non-verbal cue demonstrates that you value what he is saying.

Non-Verbal Cues

Body Language: Use open and positive body language, such as nodding, leaning slightly forward, and keeping an open posture. These cues signal that you are receptive and attentive.

Facial Expressions: Your facial expressions should reflect empathy and understanding. A warm, concerned, or encouraging look can go a long way in making your husband feel heard.

Reflective Responses

Paraphrasing: To demonstrate that you comprehend what your spouse has said, paraphrase it. Saying, "So, you're feeling frustrated because..." is one example.

Questions for clarification: Inquire to be sure you understand what he's saying. "Could you elaborate on how you felt about that?"

Validation and Empathy

Empathetic Remarks: Show empathy by recognizing his emotions. "I see how upset you are by this situation." Validate his feelings and experiences, even if you don't quite agree with them. "Considering what transpired, it makes sense that you would feel this way."

Don't Interrupt

Hold Back Reactions: Refrain from interjecting or offering ideas right away. Give him time to complete his thinking before answering.

Active Patience: Show him the time and patience he needs to completely express himself.

The Benefits of Active Listening in Romance

Enhances Emotional Intimacy

Deepens Connection: When you listen actively, it fosters a deeper emotional connection, showing your husband that you genuinely care about his thoughts and feelings.

Builds Trust: Consistent active listening builds trust as it demonstrates reliability and respect for his perspective.

Improves Communication

Reduces Misunderstandings: By actively listening, you can clarify and understand his messages better, reducing the likelihood of misunderstandings.

Encourages Open Dialogue: When your husband feels heard, he is more likely to open up and share his feelings and concerns, promoting healthier communication.

Supports Conflict Resolution

Defuses Tension: Active listening can help defuse tension during conflicts by making your husband feel respected and understood.

Fosters Compromise: Understanding his perspective through active listening makes it easier to find common ground and work towards mutually beneficial solutions.

Boosts Emotional Support

Provides Comfort: Knowing that you are truly listening can be a great source of comfort and emotional support for your husband, especially during challenging times.

Strengthens Partnership: Active listening reinforces your role as a supportive partner, enhancing the overall strength of your relationship.

Practical Tips for Effective Listening

Set Aside Regular Time for Conversations

Dedicated Time: Schedule regular times to talk without distractions. This could be during dinner, before bed, or any other time that works for both of you.

Check-Ins: Regular check-ins can help you stay connected and address any issues before they become bigger problems.

Be Present

Mindfulness: Practice mindfulness to stay present during conversations. Focus on the moment and avoid letting your mind wander.

Engage Fully: Show through your actions and words that you are fully engaged in the conversation.

Practice Patience and Open-Mindedness

Avoid Judging: Approach conversations with an open mind and avoid making judgments or jumping to conclusions.

Stay Patient: Give your husband the time and space to express himself without feeling rushed or pressured.

Use Positive Reinforcement

Acknowledge Efforts: Acknowledge and appreciate his effort to communicate, especially if it's about something difficult or personal.

Encourage Sharing: Encourage him to share by showing appreciation for his openness and honesty.

Follow Up

Show Interest: Follow up on previous conversations to show that you remember and care about what was discussed. "How did that meeting go?" or "Have you been feeling better about…?"

Stay Engaged: Staying engaged over time demonstrates ongoing support and interest in his life.

Overcoming Listening Barriers

Address Emotional Barriers

Manage Emotions: If strong emotions arise during a conversation, take a moment to calm down before continuing. Emotions can cloud your ability to listen effectively.

Practice Self-Awareness: Be aware of your own emotional triggers and how they might affect your listening abilities.

Improve Listening Skills

Seek Feedback: Ask your husband for feedback on your listening skills and be open to making improvements.

Continual Learning: Read books, attend workshops, or seek resources on effective communication and active listening to continually improve your skills.

By prioritizing active listening, you show your husband that his thoughts, feelings, and experiences matter. This practice not only strengthens your romantic relationship but also fosters a deeper, more supportive, and understanding partnership.

Expressing Your Feelings and Desires

It takes an open and sincere conversation to keep a relationship happy and healthy. Effectively communicating your needs and wants to your spouse can improve intimacy, clear up miscommunication, and build a stronger bond. This section examines the value of expressing your feelings and offers helpful methods for doing so.

Why It's Important to Express Feelings and Desires:

It Fosters Understanding and Connection

Emotional Intimacy: By letting your spouse into your inner world, communicating your wants and feelings fosters emotional intimacy.

Strengthens Bond: Open communication creates a stronger bond, fostering a sense of closeness and mutual understanding.

Prevents Resentment and Misunderstandings

Avoids Miscommunication: Clearly expressing your needs and feelings reduces the likelihood of misunderstandings that can lead to conflict.

Prevents Resentment: Holding back your feelings can lead to resentment and frustration. Openly communicating helps address issues before they escalate.

Enhances Relationship Satisfaction

Mutual Fulfillment: When both partners express their desires and needs, it leads to greater mutual satisfaction and a more balanced relationship.

Empowers Growth: Sharing your feelings and desires encourages personal and relationship growth by fostering a supportive environment for change.

Strategies for Expressing Your Feelings and Desires

Create a Safe and Open Environment

Choose the Right Time and Place: Select a comfortable and private setting for discussing important feelings and desires. Avoid times of high stress or distractions.

Ensure Emotional Safety: Approach the conversation with a non-judgmental and supportive attitude, creating a safe space for open dialogue.

Use Clear and Direct Communication

Be Specific: Express your desires and feelings clearly. Try stating something like, "I feel unheard when we talk about important issues," rather than, "You never listen to me."

Steer clear of assumptions: Don't assume your husband's motives or thoughts; instead, speak from your point of view. Make use of "I" expressions, like "I need..." or "I feel..."

Be Emotionally Sincere

Be Vulnerable: Permit yourself to be open and honest about how you really feel. Being vulnerable can strengthen your bond and promote trust.

Recognize Your Feelings: Acknowledge your feelings and communicate them openly. Tell your hubby if you're delighted, unhappy, or hurt.

Seek Comprehension and Input

Invite Questions:

Pose Queries: To make sure he grasps your viewpoint, encourage your husband to enquire. "Are you curious about my emotional state in any way?"

Request Feedback: Ask for his thoughts and feelings in response to what you've shared. This promotes a two-way dialogue and mutual understanding.

Use Positive Reinforcement

Appreciate Efforts: Acknowledge and appreciate your husband's efforts to understand and respond to your feelings and desires. Positive reinforcement encourages ongoing open communication.

Encourage Reciprocity: Foster a culture of mutual sharing by encouraging your husband to express his feelings and desires as well.

Manage Emotional Reactions

Stay Calm: If the conversation becomes emotionally charged, take a moment to calm down before continuing. Staying calm helps maintain a productive dialogue.

Be Patient: Allow time for your husband to process and respond to what you've shared. Patience fosters a more thoughtful and empathetic response.

Overcoming Barriers to Expression

Address Fear of Rejection or Judgment

Build Trust: Trust is essential for open communication. Work on building and maintaining trust through consistent, supportive actions and words.

Reassure Your Partner: Reassure your husband that your goal is to improve the relationship, not to criticize or blame.

Practice Self-Awareness and Reflection

Understand Your Emotions: Before talking to your spouse about your feelings and desires, give yourself some space to think and gain an understanding of them.

Determine Trends: Take note of any trends in the way you express and feel your emotions. Being self-aware can improve your communication skills.

Seek Expert Advice When Necessary

Couples Counselling: You might think about getting in touch with a couple's counsellor if you're having trouble communicating in a healthy way. A specialist can offer techniques and resources to enhance communication.

Individual Therapy: You can improve your understanding and expression of your emotions through individual therapy, which can lead to more positive communication in your relationship.

Practical Tips for Effective Expression

Regular Check-Ins

Scheduled Discussions: Set aside regular times to discuss your feelings and desires. These check-ins can prevent issues from building up and ensure ongoing communication.

Daily Touchpoints: Incorporate brief, daily touchpoints to share small updates on your feelings and experiences. This keeps the lines of communication open and builds a habit of sharing.

Non-Verbal Communication

Body Language: Use positive body language, such as open posture, eye contact, and gentle touch, to reinforce your words and show that you are engaged.

Tone of Voice: Pay attention to your tone of voice. A calm and gentle tone can help convey your message more effectively and reduce the risk of misunderstandings.

Journaling

Reflective Writing: Keep a journal to reflect on your feelings and desires. Writing can help you organize your thoughts and gain clarity before discussing them with your husband.

Shared Journals: Consider keeping a shared journal where both of you can write down your thoughts and feelings. This can be a non-verbal way to express emotions and foster communication.

Active Listening

Reciprocal Sharing: After expressing your feelings, actively listen to your husband's response. Show empathy and understanding, reinforcing a cycle of mutual sharing and listening.

Validation: Validate his feelings and perspectives, even if they differ from yours. Validation shows respect for his experiences and promotes open dialogue.

By expressing your feelings and desires openly and effectively, you create a foundation of trust, understanding, and emotional intimacy in your relationship. This practice not only strengthens your romantic connection but also fosters a supportive and loving partnership where both of you can thrive.

Handling Conflicts with Care

Conflict is a natural part of any relationship, but how you handle it can significantly impact your relationship's health and longevity. Addressing conflicts with care involves a combination of effective communication, empathy, and problem-solving skills. This section delves into strategies for managing conflicts constructively, ensuring that they strengthen rather than weaken your relationship with your husband.

The Nature of Conflict

Inevitable Disagreements

Different Perspectives: Conflicts often arise from differing perspectives, needs, and expectations. Accepting that disagreements are natural can help you approach them with a more constructive mindset.

Growth Opportunities: Conflicts can be opportunities for growth, understanding, and strengthening your relationship if handled properly.

Common Causes

Communication Issues: Misunderstandings, poor communication, and unmet expectations can lead to conflict.

Stress and External Factors: External stressors such as work, finances, and family issues can exacerbate conflicts within the relationship.

Unresolved Past Issues: Past grievances and unresolved issues can resurface, causing tension and conflict.

Principles of Constructive Conflict Resolution

Stay Calm and Composed

Manage Emotions: Take a moment to calm down before engaging in a discussion. Emotional regulation helps prevent escalation and promotes clearer thinking.

Breathe and Pause: Use deep breathing techniques and pauses to maintain composure during heated moments.

Use Effective Communication

I-Statements: I-sentences: Use "I" sentences to articulate your worries and convey your emotions without placing blame. Saying "I feel hurt when..." as opposed to "You always..."

Active Listening: Pay close attention, consider what your partner says, and refrain from interrupting others when you are actively listening.

Demonstrate Compassion and Understanding

Validate Emotions: Despite your disagreement, respect and validate your spouse's emotions. This promotes cooperation and demonstrates respect.

Try to Comprehend: Try to comprehend his viewpoint and the underlying causes of his emotions and behavior. Concentrate on the Problem, Not the Person Steer clear of personal attacks: Focus on the particular problem at hand instead than criticizing your husband's morality. This keeps the discussion productive.

Separate Behavior from Identity: Distinguish between your husband's actions and his identity. Critique the behavior, not the person.

Seek Common Ground

Find Shared Goals: Identify common goals or interests that you both want to achieve. This can help align your efforts and foster a sense of teamwork.

Compromise and Collaborate: Be willing to compromise and find mutually acceptable solutions. Collaboration strengthens your partnership and builds trust.

Steps for Handling Conflicts

Set the Stage for a Productive Discussion

Choose the Right Time and Place: Select a calm, private, and neutral setting to discuss the conflict. Avoid discussing sensitive issues in public or during high-stress moments.

Agree on Ground Rules: Establish ground rules for respectful communication, such as no interrupting, no name-calling, and taking breaks if needed.

Express Your Feelings and Needs

Be Honest and Direct: Clearly and honestly express your feelings and needs. Avoid vague or indirect statements that can lead to misunderstandings.

Use Specific Examples: Provide specific examples of behaviors or situations that have caused the conflict. This clarity helps your husband understand your perspective better.

Listen and Reflect

Listen Actively: Give your full attention to your husband's perspective. Show that you are listening through nodding, maintaining eye contact, and summarizing his points.

Reflect Back: Reflect back what you've heard to ensure understanding. "So, you're saying that you feel frustrated when..."

Address the Issue Constructively

Put Your Attention on Solutions: Instead of blaming, concentrate on coming up with answers. Talk about possible solutions to end the dispute and stop it from happening again.

Together, brainstorm: Together, brainstorm potential fixes while taking into account one another's requirements and preferences.

Carry out and monitor

Put Solutions into Practice: Decide on concrete steps to resolve the problem and carry them out. In order to resolve conflicts effectively, accountability is essential.

Check In Often: Make sure that the solutions that were agreed upon are still in effect and that no new problems have emerged by following up. Frequent check-ins support progress maintenance and necessary adjustments.

Practical Tips for Handling Conflict

Take Breaks When Needed

Pause and Regroup: If a discussion becomes too heated, take a break to cool down and collect your thoughts. Agree on a time to resume the conversation.

Use Time-Outs Wisely: Time-outs can prevent escalation, but ensure you return to the discussion with a calmer mindset.

Use Non-Verbal Communication

Positive Body Language: Use positive body language, such as open posture and gentle touch, to convey empathy and reduce tension.

Tone of Voice: Maintain a calm and gentle tone of voice, even when discussing difficult topics. This helps keep the conversation respectful and constructive.

Practice Conflict-Resolution Skills

Role-Playing: Practice conflict resolution through role-playing scenarios. This can help you prepare for real conflicts and develop better responses.

Learn from Experience: Reflect on past conflicts and learn from them. Identify what worked well and what didn't, and apply these lessons to future conflicts.

Focus on Long-Term Relationship Goals

Keep the Bigger Picture in Mind: Remember that conflicts are a normal part of any relationship. Focus on your long-term relationship goals and the love and commitment you share.

Celebrate Progress: Celebrate the progress you make in resolving conflicts and improving your communication. Acknowledge the effort and growth in your relationship.

Handling conflicts with care involves a combination of effective communication, empathy, and problem-solving skills. By approaching conflicts constructively, you can turn challenges into opportunities for growth and strengthen your relationship with your husband.

Building a Supportive Dialogue

A supportive dialogue is essential for maintaining a healthy, loving, and understanding relationship. It involves creating an environment where both partners feel safe, valued, and heard. This section explores strategies for fostering a supportive dialogue that promotes mutual respect, empathy, and collaboration in your relationship with your husband.

The Importance of Supportive Dialogue

Enhances Emotional Intimacy

Deepens Connection: Supportive dialogue fosters a deeper emotional connection by allowing both partners to share their thoughts and feelings openly.

Builds Trust: Consistent, supportive communication builds trust and strengthens the bond between partners.

Promotes Understanding and Empathy

Mutual Respect: A supportive dialogue encourages mutual respect and understanding, helping both partners appreciate each other's perspectives.

Reduces Misunderstandings: Clear and empathetic communication reduces the likelihood of misunderstandings and conflicts.

Encourages Collaborative Problem-Solving

Teamwork: Supportive dialogue promotes a sense of teamwork, enabling partners to work together to solve problems and address challenges.

Shared Goals: It helps align partners on shared goals and values, fostering a more cohesive and unified relationship.

Key Elements of a Supportive Dialogue

Active Listening

Full Attention: Complete Focus: During your husband's speech, give him your whole attention. This demonstrates how much you regard his feelings and opinions.

Reflective Reactions: Give back what he says to make sure you comprehend and to demonstrate your interest. For example; Saying, "I hear you saying that…"

Validation and Empathy

Embrace Emotions: Recognize and respect your spouse's emotions, even if you disagree with his viewpoint. "I recognize that you are upset about..."

Exhibit Empathy: Demonstrate empathy by placing yourself in his position and comprehending his feelings.

Honest and Transparent Communication

Transparency: Communicate your needs, feelings, and views in an honest and open manner. Openness promotes trust and lowers the possibility of miscommunication.

Clear Expression: Clearly express your feelings and desires using "I" statements to avoid sounding accusatory. "I feel… because…"

Respect and Appreciation

Respect Boundaries: Respect your husband's boundaries and privacy. This demonstrates consideration and respect for his individuality.

Show Appreciation: Regularly express appreciation for your husband's efforts, contributions, and positive qualities. Appreciation reinforces positive behavior and strengthens the relationship.

Constructive Feedback

Be Specific: Provide specific feedback rather than general criticisms. Specificity helps your husband understand exactly what behavior or action needs to change.

Positive Tone: Deliver feedback in a positive, supportive tone. Focus on solutions rather than blame.

Strategies for Building a Supportive Dialogue

Create a Safe Space for Communication

Set Ground Rules: Establish ground rules for respectful communication, such as no interrupting, no name-calling, and taking turns speaking.

Safe Environment: Ensure that your conversations take place in a comfortable, private setting where both partners feel safe to express themselves.

Regular Check-Ins

Scheduled Discussions: Schedule regular times to check in with each other about your feelings, needs, and any issues that may have arisen.

Daily Touchpoints: Incorporate brief, daily touchpoints to maintain open lines of communication and prevent issues from escalating.

Use Positive Reinforcement

Acknowledge Efforts: Acknowledge and appreciate your husband's efforts to communicate and address issues. Positive reinforcement encourages continued open dialogue.

Celebrate Little Wins: Give yourself kudos for little accomplishments and developments in your relationships and communication. This creates a happy and encouraging environment.

Exercise Understanding and Patience

Have patience: As your spouse shares his ideas and emotions with you, have patience with him. Don't rush the talk or put too much pressure on him to answer right away.

Show Understanding: Pay close attention as you listen and react with empathy to show that you understand. Gaining understanding promotes open conversation and trust. Look for points of agreement Identify Common Values: Decide on and concentrate on common goals and values. This promotes togetherness and helps you focus your efforts.

Seek Common Ground

Find Shared Values: Identify and focus on shared values and goals. This helps align your efforts and fosters a sense of unity.

Collaborative Solutions: Work together to find solutions to problems. Collaboration promotes a sense of partnership and mutual support.

Overcoming Barriers to Supportive Dialogue

Address Emotional Barriers

Manage Stress: Address external stressors that may impact your ability to communicate effectively. Stress management techniques such as exercise, meditation, and hobbies can help.

Emotional Awareness: Be aware of your own emotions and how they affect your communication. Practice emotional regulation to maintain a calm and supportive tone.

Improve Communication Skills

Learn Together: Consider taking a communication skills workshop or reading books on effective communication together. Learning together fosters mutual growth and understanding.

Practice Regularly: Regularly practice communication techniques such as active listening, empathy, and clear expression. Consistent practice leads to improvement over time.

Practical Tips for Maintaining a Supportive Dialogue

Use Non-Verbal Communication

Body Language: Use positive body language, such as open posture, eye contact, and gentle touch, to reinforce your words and show that you are engaged.

Facial Expressions: Make sure your facial expressions are consistent with what you are saying. A kind, supportive, or worried expression can help you communicate more effectively.

Incorporate Humor and Playfulness Lighten the Mood:

Use humor: Humor and playfulness to lighten the mood and make communication more enjoyable. This can help reduce tension and foster a positive atmosphere.

Shared Laughter: Find moments to laugh together and enjoy each other's company.

Reflect and Adjust Regularly: Regularly reflect on your communication patterns and the effectiveness of your dialogue. Identify areas for improvement and celebrate successes.

Be Flexible: Be willing to modify your communication strategy in response to feedback and evolving circumstances

Cultivate a Growth Mindset

Embrace Challenges: View communication challenges as opportunities for growth and learning. A growth mindset fosters resilience and a positive outlook.

Continuous Improvement: Strive for continuous improvement in your communication skills and relationship. Celebrate progress and remain committed to growth.

By building a supportive dialogue, you create an environment where both partners feel valued, understood, and connected. This foundation of mutual respect and empathy not only strengthens your romantic relationship but also fosters a deeper, more fulfilling partnership.

Chapter 3

Everyday Romantic Gestures

Showing Appreciation

Showing appreciation is a cornerstone of a healthy, thriving relationship. It strengthens the emotional bond between partners, reinforces positive behaviors, and fosters a sense of mutual respect and gratitude. This section explores the importance of showing appreciation and provides practical strategies to express gratitude and recognition in your relationship with your husband.

The Importance of Showing Appreciation

Enhances Emotional Connection

Fosters Intimacy: Regular expressions of appreciation create a deeper emotional connection by making your husband feel valued and cherished.

Strengthens Bond: Appreciation reinforces the bond between partners, reminding them of the positive qualities and actions that brought them together.

Encourages Positive Behavior

Positive Reinforcement: Recognizing and appreciating your husband's efforts and behaviors encourages him to continue those positive actions.

Boosts Morale: Appreciation boosts your husband's morale and self-esteem, making him feel good about himself and his contributions to the relationship.

Promotes a Positive Relationship Atmosphere

Reduces Negativity: Focusing on appreciation rather than criticism helps reduce negativity and conflict in the relationship.

Creates a Supportive Environment: A culture of appreciation fosters a supportive, loving environment where both partners feel encouraged and motivated.

Improves Communication

Opens Channels: Expressing appreciation opens channels of communication and makes it easier for partners to discuss their feelings and needs.

Builds Trust: Regular appreciation builds trust, as it shows that you notice and value your husband's efforts and contributions.

Strategies for Showing Appreciation

Express Verbal Appreciation

Be Specific: When expressing gratitude, be clear about the things for which you are thankful. Say something like, "Thank you for cooking dinner tonight; it was delicious," as opposed to just "Thank you."

Make Use of Positive Words: Express your gratitude by using language that is upbeat and supportive. "I'm so grateful for how you...,"

Compose letters and notes.

Handwritten Notes: Express your love and gratitude for your spouse in handwritten notes or cards that you leave. These modest deeds can make a significant difference. Love Letters: Express your gratitude and sentiments in love letters. This might be an effective method to communicate intense feelings and fortify your relationship.

Show Physical Affection

Hugs and Kisses: Physical affection, such as hugs, kisses, and gentle touches, can convey appreciation and reinforce your emotional connection.

Intimate Gestures: Intimate gestures, like holding hands or cuddling, can also be powerful expressions of appreciation and love.

Acts of Service

Help with Tasks: Show appreciation by helping with tasks or chores that your husband usually handles. This demonstrates your recognition of his efforts.

Special Treats: Plan special treats or surprises, such as preparing his favorite meal or organizing a fun outing, to show your appreciation.

Celebrate Achievements and Milestones

Acknowledge Successes: Celebrate your husband's achievements, both big and small. Acknowledge his hard work and success in his personal and professional life.

Mark Special Occasions: Celebrate special occasions, such as anniversaries, birthdays, and significant milestones, with thoughtful gestures and expressions of appreciation.

Quality Time

Spend Time Together: Dedicate quality time to spend together, doing activities that you both enjoy. This shows that you value and appreciate his company.

Listen Actively: Show appreciation by actively listening to your husband when he talks about his day, interests, or concerns. Being present and engaged demonstrates your appreciation for him.

Public Acknowledgment

Share with Others: Publicly acknowledge your husband's positive qualities and efforts in front of family and friends. This can boost his confidence and show your pride in him.

Social media: Use social media to share your appreciation, if comfortable, by posting about your husband's achievements and expressing your gratitude.

Overcoming Barriers to Showing Appreciation

Address Emotional Barriers

Self-Reflection: Reflect on any emotional barriers that may prevent you from expressing appreciation, such as resentment or unspoken grievances. Addressing these issues can help open the path to genuine appreciation.

Focus on Positives: Shift your focus from negative aspects of your relationship to the positive qualities and actions of your husband. This change in perspective can make it easier to show appreciation.

Develop a Habit of Gratitude

Daily Gratitude Practice: Incorporate a daily gratitude practice where you take time to reflect on and acknowledge the things you appreciate about your husband.

Gratitude Journal: Keep a gratitude journal where you regularly write down things you appreciate about your husband and your relationship. This can help reinforce a habit of appreciation.

Communicate Your Needs

Open Dialogue: Have an open dialogue with your husband about the importance of appreciation in your relationship. Discuss how you both can better express gratitude and recognition.

Seek Feedback: Ask for feedback on how you can improve in showing appreciation. This demonstrates your commitment to enhancing your relationship.

Be Consistent and Sincere

Consistency: Make showing appreciation a consistent practice rather than a one-time effort. Regular expressions of gratitude have a more significant impact.

Sincerity: Ensure that your expressions of appreciation are genuine and sincere. Authenticity is key to building trust and emotional connection.

Practical Tips for Showing Appreciation

Start and End the Day with Gratitude

Morning Appreciation: Begin the day by thanking your spouse for something he accomplished or for a trait you find admirable. This makes the day's vibe upbeat. **Evening Thought:** Conclude the day by thinking back on and mentioning something you valued about your spouse that particular day. Positive connections are reinforced in this way.

Establish an Appreciation Culture

Model Behavior: Set a good example by expressing gratitude on a regular basis. This may inspire your spouse to follow suit.

Promote Mutual Appreciation: Talk about and share the things you have in common with your partner on a frequent basis to cultivate a culture of mutual appreciation.

Use Technology

Send Texts: Send appreciative texts or messages throughout the day to let your husband know you are thinking of him and appreciate his efforts.

Digital Notes: Use digital notes or apps to leave virtual notes of appreciation. These can be a convenient way to express gratitude, especially when apart.

Incorporate Appreciation into Daily Routines

Mealtime Gratitude: Use mealtimes as an opportunity to express appreciation. Share things you are grateful for about each other during dinner.

Bedtime Rituals: Make expressing appreciation a part of your bedtime routine. Share a positive thought or gratitude before going to sleep.

By consistently showing appreciation, you create a nurturing and loving environment that enhances your relationship. These expressions of gratitude not only strengthen your emotional connection but also promote a positive, supportive, and fulfilling partnership with your husband.

Acts of Service and Kindness

Acts of service and kindness are powerful expressions of love and appreciation in a relationship. These actions demonstrate your commitment to your partner's well-being and happiness, reinforcing the emotional bond between you. This section explores the importance of acts of service and kindness and provides practical strategies for incorporating them into your relationship with your husband.

The Importance of Acts of Service and Kindness

Demonstrates Love and Commitment

Actions Speak Louder: Acts of service and kindness show your love and commitment through tangible actions, reinforcing your emotional connection.

Shows Dedication: These actions demonstrate your dedication to making your husband's life easier and more enjoyable, highlighting your commitment to the relationship.

Enhances Emotional Intimacy

Builds Trust: Regular acts of service build trust and reliability, as your husband sees that you are dependable and attentive to his needs.

Deepens Connection: Acts of kindness deepen your emotional connection by fostering a sense of security and mutual support.

Encourages Positive Behavior

Reciprocity: Acts of service often inspire reciprocal actions, creating a positive cycle of kindness and support in the relationship.

Promotes Gratitude: Regular acts of kindness promote a sense of gratitude and appreciation, contributing to a more positive relationship atmosphere.

Strengthens Partnership

Teamwork: Performing acts of service fosters a sense of teamwork and collaboration, reinforcing the idea that you are working together toward common goals.

Reduces Stress: Helping each other with daily tasks and challenges reduces stress and creates a more harmonious living environment.

Strategies for Acts of Service and Kindness

Identify His Needs and Preferences

Understand His Love Language: Determine if acts of service are a primary love language for your husband. If so, these actions will be especially meaningful to him.

Ask and Observe: Ask your husband about his preferences and observe what tasks or actions he appreciates the most. Tailor your acts of service to his specific needs.

Help with Daily Tasks

Household Chores: Assist with household chores such as cleaning, cooking, laundry, and yard work. Sharing these responsibilities shows your support and reduces his workload.

Errands: Run errands for your husband, such as grocery shopping, picking up dry cleaning, or handling administrative tasks. This demonstrates your willingness to help with practical needs.

Support His Goals and Interests

Encourage Hobbies: Support your husband's hobbies and interests by helping him find time for them, providing necessary resources, or participating with him.

Career Support: Show support for his career goals by helping with tasks that free up his time, offering encouragement, or assisting with job-related projects.

Offer Emotional Support

Be Present: Offer a listening ear and emotional support during stressful times. Your presence and empathy can be incredibly comforting.

Encourage Self-Care: Encourage your husband to take care of himself by suggesting and supporting activities that promote his well-being, such as exercise, hobbies, or relaxation.

Plan Thoughtful Surprises

Special Treats: Plan small surprises such as his favorite meal, a special dessert, or a relaxing bath to show that you're thinking of him.

Romantic Gestures: Organize romantic gestures like a surprise date night, a handwritten love note, or a spontaneous outing to keep the romance alive.

Show Appreciation Through Actions

Celebrate Achievements: Celebrate your husband's achievements with thoughtful actions, such as organizing a small celebration, giving a meaningful gift, or planning a special day.

Daily Acts of Kindness: Incorporate daily acts of kindness, like making his coffee in the morning, packing his lunch, or preparing his favorite snack.

Be Attentive to His Well-Being

Health and Wellness: Encourage and support healthy habits by cooking nutritious meals, planning active outings, or reminding him to take breaks and relax.

Comfort and Care: Provide comfort and care when he's feeling unwell, whether through making him soup, ensuring he rests, or handling his responsibilities.

Overcoming Barriers to Acts of Service and Kindness

Address Emotional Barriers

Self-Reflection: Reflect on any emotional barriers that may prevent you from performing acts of service, such as past resentments or feelings of imbalance. Address these issues to foster a more giving mindset.

Focus on Positivity: Shift your focus from negative aspects of your relationship to the positive impact of your actions.

This change in perspective can make it easier to perform acts of kindness.

Develop a Habit of Service

Consistent Practice: Make acts of service a regular part of your routine. Consistency helps build a habit and makes these actions feel more natural.

Set Intentions: Set daily or weekly intentions to perform specific acts of service for your husband. This keeps you focused and committed to showing kindness.

Communicate Your Efforts

Open Dialogue: Discuss your efforts with your husband and let him know you're trying to be more supportive. This can encourage mutual appreciation and understanding.

Seek Feedback: Ask for feedback on how your acts of service are received and if there are specific areas where he would appreciate more support.

Balance Giving and Receiving

Mutual Support: Ensure that acts of service and kindness are mutual. Encourage your husband to also participate in this positive cycle, fostering a balanced and supportive relationship.

Self-Care: Take care of your own needs as well. A balanced approach ensures that you have the energy and motivation to continue being supportive.

Practical Tips for Acts of Service and Kindness

Start Small

Small Gestures: Begin with small, manageable gestures of kindness, such as making his favorite breakfast or taking out the trash without being asked.

Build Gradually: Gradually increase the frequency and significance of your acts of service as they become a natural part of your routine.

Be Creative

Think Outside the Box: Get creative with your acts of service. Consider what would genuinely surprise and delight your husband, and tailor your actions to his unique preferences.

Personal Touches: Add personal touches to your acts of kindness to make them more meaningful. For example, prepare a meal with ingredients you know he loves or create a custom playlist for his commute.

Use Technology

Digital Reminders: Use technology to set reminders for acts of service, such as sending a thoughtful text, preparing a surprise, or completing a task.

Online Resources: Leverage online resources for inspiration, such as finding new recipes to cook for him, planning a special date, or organizing a surprise delivery.

Reflect and Adjust

Regular Self-Reflection: Consider your deeds of kindness and how they have affected your relationship. Determine what is effective and what needs to be improved.

Be Adaptable: Show that you're prepared to change course in response to your husband's input and evolving requirements. Being adaptable guarantees that your work will always be valued and relevant.

Develop an Attitude of Gratitude

Practice Gratitude: Make it a habit to be grateful for your spouse and your partnership on a regular basis. This style of thinking encourages an innate desire to do good deeds.

Adopt Generosity: In all facets of your relationship, adopt a generous mindset. Your emotional connection and overall relationship happiness are improved when you adopt a giving perspective.

You may build a caring, supportive environment in your relationship that strengthens your emotional connection and fosters mutual appreciation by integrating acts of kindness and service.

Thoughtful Surprises

Thoughtful surprises are a wonderful way to show your husband that you care and are thinking about him. They can add excitement and romance to your relationship, helping to keep the spark alive. This section explores the importance of thoughtful surprises and provides practical ideas and strategies to incorporate them into your relationship.

The Importance of Thoughtful Surprises

Keeps the Romance Alive

Excitement: Surprises add an element of excitement and novelty to the relationship, preventing it from becoming routine or monotonous.

Spontaneity: They bring spontaneity, which is often associated with the early stages of romance, helping to rekindle those initial feelings of love and attraction.

Shows Appreciation and Thoughtfulness

Personalized Gestures: Thoughtful surprises demonstrate that you pay attention to your husband's likes, dislikes, and needs, showing him that you truly care.

Effort and Consideration: They reflect the effort and consideration you put into making him happy, reinforcing your appreciation and love.

Strengthens Emotional Connection

Shared Joy: Surprises create moments of shared joy and happiness, strengthening your emotional connection and creating lasting memories.

Positive Reinforcement: They reinforce positive feelings and interactions, contributing to a more loving and supportive relationship atmosphere.

Enhances Communication and Understanding

Encourages Dialogue: Surprises can open up opportunities for communication and discussions about what makes each other happy.

Understanding Preferences: Planning surprises helps you understand your husband's preferences and desires more deeply, fostering better mutual understanding.

Ideas for Thoughtful Surprises

Personalized Gifts

Custom Items: Gift your husband personalized items, such as a custom-engraved watch, a monogrammed wallet, or a photo book of your favorite memories together.

Hobby-Related Gifts: Consider gifts related to his hobbies or interests, such as a special edition book by his favorite author, new gear for his favorite sport, or tools for his DIY projects.

Unexpected Acts of Kindness

Breakfast in Bed: Surprise him with breakfast in bed on a weekend morning, complete with his favorite dishes.

Household Help: Take care of a chore or task he typically handles without being asked, showing your appreciation for his efforts.

Romantic Gestures

Love Notes: Leave small love notes in places he'll find throughout the day, such as his wallet, car, or lunch bag.

Candlelit Dinner: Plan a surprise candlelit dinner at home or at a favorite restaurant, complete with his favorite foods and drinks.

Plan a Surprise Date or Outing

Mystery Date: Organize a mystery date where you plan all the details and keep the destination a secret until you arrive.

Adventure Day: Plan a day filled with activities he enjoys, such as hiking, visiting a museum, or going to a sports event.

Surprise Getaways

Weekend Trip: Arrange a weekend getaway to a destination he loves or has always wanted to visit. Plan all the details, including accommodations, activities, and dining.

Staycation: If travel isn't feasible, plan a staycation with fun activities at home or nearby, such as a spa day, movie marathon, or exploring local attractions.

Thoughtful Daily Gestures

Special Treats: Surprise him with his favorite snack, drink, or dessert after a long day.

Unexpected Compliments: Give him unexpected compliments or words of affirmation to boost his mood and show your appreciation.

Surprise Celebrations

Achievement Celebration: Celebrate his achievements, whether big or small, with a surprise party, special dinner, or thoughtful gift.

Anniversary Surprises: Plan unique surprises for your anniversaries, such as recreating your first date, writing a heartfelt letter, or giving a meaningful gift.

Strategies for Planning Thoughtful Surprises

Know His Preferences

Listen and Observe: Ways to Arrange Thoughtful Surprises Recognize His Preferences

Pay attention and take note: Observe his hobbies, dislikes, and likes. Pay attention to what he says and see how he responds in various circumstances.

Ask Inconspicuously: Without disclosing your plans, inquire informally about his preferences or wish list items.
Make a Plan

Set Reminders: Arrange surprises for particular days or occasions by using calendar notes or reminders. Be Ready: To make sure everything goes as planned, gather all required supplies or make reservations ahead of time.

Be Inventive and Free-spirited

Be Creative and Spontaneous

Think Outside the Box: Get creative with your surprises. Consider what would truly delight and surprise him.

Embrace Spontaneity: While planning is important, leave room for spontaneous surprises that can add an extra layer of excitement.

Pay Attention to Timing

Choose the Right Moment: Pick a time when he can fully enjoy and appreciate the surprise, avoiding moments of stress or busyness.

Consider His Schedule: Ensure the surprise fits into his schedule and doesn't conflict with his commitments or responsibilities.

Personalize Your Approach

Tailor to His Interests: Customize the surprise to align with his personal interests and preferences for maximum impact.

Add Personal Touches: Incorporate personal touches, such as inside jokes, shared memories, or sentimental elements.

Overcoming Barriers to Thoughtful Surprises

Address Practical Challenges

Budget-Friendly Options: Thoughtful surprises don't have to be expensive. Focus on meaningful gestures that fit within your budget.

Time Management: Plan surprises that fit into your schedule and allow you to balance other responsibilities.

Maintain Balance

Mutual Effort: Encourage a mutual exchange of surprises and thoughtful gestures to maintain balance and prevent one-sided efforts.

Avoid Overdoing: While surprises are wonderful, avoid overdoing them to the point where they lose their special impact.

Communicate and Understand

Clarify Expectations: Have open discussions about each other's expectations and preferences regarding surprises and romantic gestures.

Be Receptive: Be receptive to feedback and willing to adjust your approach based on his responses and preferences.

Manage Expectations

Keep It Realistic: Ensure that your surprises are realistic and achievable, avoiding overly complex plans that may cause stress or disappointment.

Appreciate the Effort: Focus on the effort and thought behind the surprise rather than perfection. Even simple gestures can have a profound impact.

Practical Tips for Thoughtful Surprises

Utilize Special Occasions

Birthdays and Anniversaries: Use special occasions as opportunities to plan more elaborate surprises that celebrate your relationship milestones.

Ordinary Days: Don't wait for special occasions—surprise him on ordinary days to show that you're thinking of him all the time.

Involve Friends and Family

Collaborative Surprises: Involve friends and family in planning and executing surprises, especially for bigger events or celebrations.

Surprise Gatherings: Organize surprise gatherings with loved ones for added joy and shared happiness.

Document the Moments

Capture Memories: Take photos or videos of the surprise moments to create lasting memories that you can both look back on.

Create Keepsakes: Consider creating keepsakes or mementos from the surprises, such as a scrapbook, photo album, or memory jar.

Reflect and Learn

Reflect on Impact: Reflect on the impact of your surprises and what resonated most with your husband. Use this insight for future planning.

Continuous Improvement: Continuously improve your approach to surprises by learning from each experience and incorporating new ideas.

By incorporating thoughtful surprises into your relationship, you can maintain excitement, deepen your emotional connection, and show your husband that you cherish and appreciate him. These gestures, whether big or small, play a crucial role in keeping the romance alive and fostering a loving, supportive partnership.

Making Time for Each Other

In the hustle and bustle of everyday life, it's easy for couples to get caught up in their individual responsibilities and lose sight of the importance of spending quality time together. Making time for each other is crucial for maintaining a strong, healthy relationship. This section explores the significance of prioritizing time together and offers practical strategies for ensuring that you and your husband stay connected.

The Importance of Making Time for Each Other

Strengthens Emotional Connection

Bonding: Spending quality time together strengthens your emotional bond, allowing you to reconnect and deepen your understanding of each other.

Shared Experiences: Creating shared experiences and memories fosters a sense of unity and reinforces your partnership.

Improves Communication

Open Dialogue: Regularly setting aside time for each other encourages open and honest communication, helping to address issues before they escalate.

Active Listening: Dedicated time together allows for active listening, ensuring that both partners feel heard and valued.

Enhances Relationship Satisfaction

Mutual Enjoyment: Engaging in enjoyable activities together boosts overall relationship satisfaction and happiness.

Romantic Connection: Prioritizing time for each other keeps the romantic spark alive, maintaining the excitement and passion in your relationship.

Supports Personal and Mutual Growth

Personal Fulfillment: Spending time together supports individual growth by fostering a supportive environment where both partners can pursue their interests and goals.

Shared Goals: Working on shared goals and projects strengthens your partnership and creates a sense of shared purpose.

Strategies for Making Time for Each Other

Schedule Regular Date Nights

Consistent Routine: Establish a regular date night routine, whether it's weekly, bi-weekly, or monthly. Consistency ensures that you prioritize your relationship despite busy schedules.

Variety: Mix up your date night activities to keep things interesting. Try new restaurants, visit different places, or engage in various activities to create new experiences together.

Plan Quality Time at Home

Home Dates: Plan at-home dates, such as cooking a meal together, having a movie night, or playing board games. These activities can be as enjoyable as going out and are often more convenient.

Unplugged Time: Dedicate time at home where you both disconnect from electronic devices and focus solely on each other.

Create Daily Rituals

Morning and Evening Routines: Establish morning and evening routines that include time for each other. This could be enjoying a cup of coffee together in the morning or sharing a moment of reflection before bed.

Check-Ins: Incorporate daily check-ins where you take a few minutes to talk about your day, share your thoughts, and connect emotionally.

Take Mini Breaks

Lunch Dates: If your schedules allow, meet for lunch during the workday to spend some time together.

Walks and Outings: Take short walks or outings together during the day, providing an opportunity to reconnect and enjoy each other's company.

Plan Weekend Getaways

Short Trips: Plan weekend getaways to nearby destinations. These short trips can provide a refreshing change of scenery and dedicated time for each other.

Staycations: If travel isn't feasible, plan a staycation where you enjoy local activities or create a vacation-like experience at home.

Engage in Shared Hobbies and Interests

Common Activities: Identify hobbies and interests that you both enjoy and make time to engage in them together. This could include cooking, gardening, sports, or arts and crafts.

Learn Together: Take up a new hobby or activity together, such as a dance class, cooking course, or fitness routine. Learning something new together can be a bonding experience.

Support Each Other's Individual Interests

Encourage Participation: Show interest in each other's hobbies and support participation. Join your husband in his activities and invite him to join you in yours.

Balance: Find a balance between spending time together and allowing for individual pursuits, ensuring that both partners feel fulfilled and supported.

Overcoming Barriers to Making Time for Each Other

Address Busy Schedules

Prioritize Time: Make your relationship a priority by scheduling time together as you would any other important commitment. Block out time on your calendar to ensure it happens.

Time Management: Improve time management skills to create more free time. Delegate tasks, set boundaries, and streamline routines to make room for quality time together.

Communicate Needs and Expectations

Open Discussion: Have an open discussion about the importance of spending time together and how you can both make it a priority. Share your needs and expectations.

Compromise: Be willing to compromise and find solutions that work for both of you. Flexibility and understanding are key to overcoming scheduling conflicts.

Manage Stress and Fatigue

Self-Care: Prioritize self-care to manage stress and fatigue. When both partners are well-rested and less stressed, it's easier to make time for each other.

Relaxation Activities: Incorporate relaxation activities into your time together, such as taking a bath, meditating, or enjoying a quiet evening, to recharge and connect.

Create a Supportive Environment

Encourage Mutual Support: Foster a supportive environment where both partners encourage each other to prioritize the relationship and make time for each other.

Shared Responsibilities: Share household and family responsibilities to ensure that both partners have the time and energy to spend together.

Practical Tips for Making Time for Each Other

Be Present and Engaged

Active Listening: When you spend time together, engage in active listening. Be genuinely curious in your husband's feelings and thoughts.

Prioritize Quality Over Quantity: Pay more attention to the nature of your conversations than the amount of time you spend together. Spending time together in a meaningful way is more important than just being there.

Honor accomplishments and milestones

Special Occasions: Set aside time to celebrate milestones like anniversaries and birthdays. Create a memorable event to commemorate these achievements.

Little Victories: Celebrate and give thanks for the little things you've done in life. These acknowledgement moments deepen your relationship.

Be Spontaneous

Surprise Outings: Plan spontaneous outings or activities without prior notice. Surprise your husband with a date night or an unexpected adventure.

Random Acts of Kindness: Perform random acts of kindness to show your love and appreciation. These gestures can be small but meaningful.

Reflect and Adjust

Regular Check-Ins: Regularly check in with each other about how you're feeling and whether you're spending enough quality time together. Adjust your approach as needed.

Continuous Improvement: Continuously look for ways to improve your time together. Be open to trying new activities and finding better ways to connect.

By making time for each other, you invest in the health and happiness of your relationship. Prioritizing quality time together strengthens your emotional connection, enhances communication, and keeps the romance alive. These efforts create a loving, supportive partnership where both partners feel valued and cherished.

Chapter 4

Creating Memorable Experiences

Planning Date Nights He'll Love

Date nights are an essential part of maintaining a vibrant and romantic relationship. They provide an opportunity to reconnect, enjoy each other's company, and create lasting memories. This section will explore how to plan date nights that your husband will love, offering practical ideas and strategies to make each outing special and enjoyable.

The Importance of Date Nights

Rekindles Romance

Maintains Connection: Regular date nights help maintain the romantic connection, keeping the spark alive in your relationship.

Excitement and Novelty: Introducing new activities and experiences prevents the relationship from becoming monotonous, adding excitement and novelty.

Strengthens Emotional Bond

Quality Time: Spending dedicated time together strengthens your emotional bond, fostering a deeper sense of intimacy and understanding.

Shared Experiences: Creating shared memories through enjoyable activities reinforces your partnership and unity.

Improves Communication

Open Dialogue: Date nights provide a relaxed setting for open and honest conversations, helping to address any issues and improve communication.

Focused Attention: With fewer distractions, you can give each other your full attention, enhancing the quality of your interactions.

Enhances Relationship Satisfaction

Mutual Enjoyment: Engaging in fun and enjoyable activities together boosts overall relationship satisfaction and happiness.

Romantic Connection: Date nights foster a sense of romantic connection, maintaining the excitement and passion in your relationship.

Strategies for Planning Date Nights He'll Love

Consider His Interests and Hobbies

Hobby-Related Activities: Plan date nights around your husband's hobbies and interests. Whether it's sports, music, art, or outdoor activities, tailoring the date to his preferences will make it more enjoyable.

Try New Activities Together: Encourage him to try new activities that he's expressed interest in. This not only keeps things exciting but also shows that you're attentive to his desires.

Mix Up the Routine

Variety: Avoid falling into a date night routine. Mix up your activities to keep things fresh and exciting. Alternate between different types of dates, such as outdoor adventures, cultural experiences, and cozy nights in.

Surprise Elements: Add surprise elements to your dates. Whether it's a surprise location or an unexpected activity, surprises can add an element of excitement.

Create a Relaxed Atmosphere

Low-Stress Planning: Ensure that your date nights are relaxed and low-stress. Avoid overly complicated plans that might cause anxiety or fatigue.

Comfortable Settings: Choose settings that are comfortable and conducive to relaxation and enjoyment. Whether it's a quiet restaurant, a cozy café, or a scenic park, the environment should be enjoyable for both of you.

Plan Ahead

Advance Reservations: Make reservations in advance for popular venues or activities to avoid last-minute stress and ensure a smooth experience.

Logistics: Plan the logistics of your date, including transportation, timing, and any necessary arrangements, to ensure everything goes smoothly.

Focus on Shared Experiences

Team Activities: Choose activities that require teamwork and collaboration, such as cooking a meal together, solving an escape room, or participating in a friendly competition.

Memory-Making: Focus on creating lasting memories. Consider activities that are unique or meaningful, such as visiting a place where you first met or doing something that holds sentimental value.

Date Night Ideas

Outdoor Adventures

Hiking and Nature Walks: Plan a hiking trip or a nature walk in a scenic location. Pack a picnic and enjoy the beauty of the outdoors together.

Camping: Organize a camping trip where you can spend quality time in nature, enjoying activities like fishing, stargazing, and campfire cooking.

Cultural Experiences

Museum and Gallery Visits: Visit a museum or art gallery to explore new exhibits and share your thoughts and impressions.

Theater and Concerts: Attend a theater performance, concert, or live show to enjoy a cultural experience together.

Food and Drink

Cooking Classes: Enroll in a cooking class to learn new culinary skills together. Choose a cuisine you both love or are interested in exploring.

Food Tours: Go on a food tour in your city, exploring different restaurants, food trucks, or markets to try new dishes and flavors.

Recreational Activities

Sports Events: Attend a live sports event of his favorite team or sport. Share in the excitement and enjoy the atmosphere.

Bowling and Mini-Golf: Bowling and Mini-Golf: Visit a mini-golf or bowling alley for a playful and enjoyable date. An additional dimension of fun can be added by friendly competition.

Enchanting Evenings

Candlelit Dinners: Arrange a dinner at your favorite restaurant or at home under the stars. Make an effort to create a cozy and romantic ambiance.

Stargazing: Take an evening to spend stargazing in a peaceful location away from city lights. For a memorable evening, pack a blanket, some food, and maybe a telescope.

Unique and Memorable Experiences

Hot Air Balloon Ride: Experience the thrill and romance of a hot air balloon ride. Enjoy the breathtaking views and the sense of adventure.

Escape Rooms: Test your problem-solving skills together in an escape room. Working as a team to solve puzzles and find your way out can be a fun and bonding experience.

DIY Date Nights

Home Spa Night: Create a spa experience at home with massages, facials, and relaxing music. Pamper each other and unwind together.

Movie Marathon: Have a movie marathon with his favorite films or a series you both enjoy. Prepare snacks and create a cozy atmosphere for a relaxed night in.

Overcoming Barriers to Planning Date Nights

Busy Schedules

Set a Regular Schedule: Commit to a regular date night schedule, whether it's weekly, bi-weekly, or monthly. Mark it on your calendar to ensure it becomes a priority.

Flexible Planning: Be flexible with your planning. If something comes up, reschedule rather than cancel your date night.

Budget Constraints

Budget-Friendly Options: Plan budget-friendly date nights, such as picnics, home-cooked dinners, or free local events. The focus should be on spending quality time together, not on spending money.

Savings Plan: Set aside a small amount of money regularly to fund special date nights or activities that might require a bit more investment.

Lack of Ideas

Research and Inspiration: Look for inspiration online, through friends, or in local event listings. Keep a list of date night ideas that you can refer to when planning.

Try New Things: Have an open mind and a willingness to try out new things. This keeps things interesting and lets you both find new hobbies.

Distinct Passions

Balance and Compromise: Strike a balance between his and your interests. Switch between activities that suit each partner's tastes to make sure they both feel important and included.

Common Interests: Pay attention to things that you both find enjoyable. Establishing common ground might result in more meaningful and joyful date nights.

Practical Tips for Successful Date Nights

Communicate and Plan Together

Discuss Preferences: Have an open discussion about what each of you enjoys and what you'd like to do for date nights. This ensures that both partners are excited about the plans.

Collaborative Planning: Plan date nights together to ensure that they cater to both of your interests and preferences.

Be Present and Engaged

Quality Interaction: Focus on quality interaction during your date night. Avoid distractions like phones and other devices to ensure you're fully present.

Show Interest: Show genuine interest in the activities and in each other. Ask questions, share thoughts, and actively participate in the experience.

Reflect and Improve

Feedback Loop: After each date night, discuss what you both enjoyed and what could be improved. Use this feedback to plan even better date nights in the future.

Keep a Journal: Consider keeping a date night journal where you record your experiences and any memorable moments. This can be a fun way to reflect on your time together and plan future dates.

Celebrate the Effort

Appreciate Planning: Acknowledge and appreciate the effort put into planning date nights, whether it's by you or your husband. Gratitude fosters a positive atmosphere and encourages continued effort.

Celebrate Successes: Celebrate successful date nights and the positive impact they have on your relationship. Recognizing the value of these moments reinforces their importance.

By planning date nights that cater to your husband's interests and preferences, you create opportunities for meaningful connection and enjoyment. These shared experiences strengthen your bond, enhance communication, and keep the romance alive, ensuring a healthy and happy relationship.

Celebrating Special Occasions

Celebrating special occasions with your husband is a wonderful way to show your love and appreciation, create cherished memories, and strengthen your bond. Whether it's a birthday, anniversary, or a personal milestone, these moments provide an opportunity to make your husband feel valued and cherished.

The Importance of Celebrating Special Occasions

Shows Appreciation and Love

Recognition: Celebrating special occasions shows your husband that you recognize and appreciate important moments in his life.

Affirmation: It reaffirms your love and commitment, demonstrating that you value the relationship and his happiness.

Strengthens Emotional Connection

Shared Joy: Sharing joyous moments together strengthens your emotional connection and fosters a deeper sense of intimacy.

Positive Memories: Creating positive memories during special occasions reinforces the bond between you and your husband.

Enhances Relationship Satisfaction

Happiness and Fulfillment: Celebrating milestones and achievements contributes to overall relationship satisfaction and happiness.

Romantic Gesture: These celebrations are romantic gestures that keep the excitement and passion alive in your relationship.

Acknowledges Growth and Progress

Personal and Mutual Achievements: Celebrating special occasions acknowledges personal and mutual achievements, encouraging growth and progress in your relationship.

Milestones: It highlights significant milestones, providing an opportunity to reflect on your journey together.

Strategies for Celebrating Special Occasions

Personalize the Celebration

Tailored to His Preferences: Plan celebrations that reflect your husband's interests and preferences. Consider his favorite activities, foods, and hobbies.

Unique Touches: Add unique touches that make the celebration special and meaningful. Personalization shows that you've put thought and effort into the occasion.

Plan Ahead

Advance Preparation: Start planning well in advance to ensure that all details are taken care of. This reduces stress and allows for a smoother celebration.

Reservations and Bookings: Make necessary reservations and bookings early, especially for popular venues or activities, to avoid last-minute disappointments.

Surprise Elements

Unexpected Surprises: Incorporate surprise elements to add excitement and delight to the celebration. Surprises can be small or grand, but they should be thoughtful and considerate.

Secret Planning: If planning a surprise, keep the details a secret and enlist the help of friends or family if needed.

Meaningful Gifts

Thoughtful Gifts: Choose gifts that are thoughtful and meaningful. Consider his interests, needs, and desires when selecting a gift.

Personalized Items: Personalized items, such as custom-made gifts or items with sentimental value, can make the occasion even more special.

Ideas for Celebrating Special Occasions

Birthdays

Surprise Party: Plan a surprise party for your close friends and family members. Decorate the space with his preferred color schemes and themes.

Special evening: Make a gourmet meal at home or arrange a special evening at his favorite restaurant. Take into account serving a handcrafted birthday cake.

Adventure Day: Arrange a day filled with all of his favorite things to do, including going boating, hiking, or visiting an amusement park.

Romantic break for Anniversaries: Arrange a romantic break to a place you both adore. Emphasize romance and leisure whether you're travelling to a city getaway, a beach resort, or a lodge in the mountains.

Memory Lane: Relive your first date or explore sites that hold special meaning for you two. This journey back in time can be deeply meaningful and romantic

Personal Vows: Write and exchange personal vows or love letters. Reflecting on your journey together and expressing your love can be incredibly touching.

Milestones and Achievements

Career Achievements: Celebrate promotions, awards, or other career achievements with a special dinner, a toast, or a congratulatory gift.

Personal Milestones: Acknowledge personal milestones, such as completing a marathon, graduating from a course, or achieving a personal goal, with a meaningful celebration.

Joint Accomplishments: Celebrate joint accomplishments, such as buying a house, completing a project, or reaching a shared goal. Plan a celebration that acknowledges your teamwork and partnership.

Holidays

Festive Celebrations: Plan festive celebrations for holidays like Christmas, New Year's, or Valentine's Day. Decorate your home, prepare special meals, and create a joyful atmosphere.

Traditions: Establish and maintain holiday traditions that you both enjoy. Traditions provide a sense of continuity and shared joy.

Quality Time: Make an effort to spend time with each other well over the holidays. Take part in things that make you both happy and help you feel closer to one another.

Getting Past Obstacles to Enjoying Special Occasions Tight Schedules

Time management: Make special occasions a priority in your calendar. To guarantee you have time to celebrate without feeling hurried or pressured, make a plan in advance.

Flexible Celebrations: Arrange a celebration that works with your schedules if you're both very busy. A modest yet meaningful celebration does not have to be huge.

Budget Constraints

Budget-Friendly Ideas: Plan budget-friendly celebrations that are still meaningful. A homemade dinner, a heartfelt letter, or a day spent together can be just as special as an extravagant celebration.

Saving Up: Save up in advance for special occasions if you want to plan something more elaborate. Setting aside a small amount regularly can make a big difference.

Different Preferences

Compromise and Balance: Find a balance between your preferences and his. Compromise on activities and plans to ensure both partners enjoy the celebration.

Shared Decision-Making: Involve your husband in the planning process. Discuss how he'd like to celebrate and make decisions together.

Practical Tips for Memorable Celebrations

Capture the Moments

Photos and Videos: Take photos and videos to capture the special moments. These can be wonderful memories to look back on in the future.

Memory Book: Create a memory book or scrapbook to document your celebrations. Include photos, mementos, and notes about the occasion.

Focus on the Experience

Presence and Engagement: Be fully present and engaged during the celebration. Avoid distractions and focus on enjoying the time together.

Create a Relaxed Atmosphere: Ensure that the celebration is relaxed and enjoyable. Avoid overcomplicating plans that might cause stress.

Reflect and Appreciate

Reflection: Take time to reflect on the occasion and what it means to both of you. Share your thoughts and feelings with each other.

Gratitude: Express gratitude for each other and for the special moments you've shared. Acknowledging the effort and thoughtfulness behind the celebration enhances its meaning.

Continuous Improvement

Feedback Loop: After the celebration, discuss what you both enjoyed and what could be improved for future occasions. Use this feedback to plan even better celebrations.

Evolving Traditions: Allow your celebration traditions to evolve over time. Adapt to new circumstances and incorporate new ideas to keep things fresh and exciting.

Celebrating special occasions with your husband is a powerful way to show your love, create lasting memories, and strengthen your bond. By personalizing the celebrations, planning ahead, and focusing on meaningful experiences, you can make each occasion truly special and memorable.

Fun and Adventurous Activities

Engaging in fun and adventurous activities is a fantastic way to inject excitement, variety, and joy into your relationship. These activities can help you create unforgettable memories, strengthen your bond, and provide a shared sense of accomplishment and thrill.

The Importance of Fun and Adventurous Activities

Creates Lasting Memories

Unique Experiences: Engaging in adventurous activities creates unique and memorable experiences that you can look back on fondly.

Storytelling: These activities often result in great stories and anecdotes that you can share with friends and family.

Strengthens Bond and Teamwork

Shared Challenges: Tackling challenges together fosters teamwork and collaboration, strengthening your bond.

Support and Encouragement: Supporting and encouraging each other during adventurous activities enhances mutual trust and confidence.

Enhances Relationship Excitement

Breaks Routine: Fun and adventurous activities break the monotony of daily routines, adding excitement and novelty to your relationship.

Shared Joy: The thrill and joy of adventure create positive emotions and a sense of exhilaration that you share as a couple.

Promotes Personal and Mutual Growth

Personal Development: Engaging in new and challenging activities promotes personal growth, resilience, and self-confidence.

Shared Achievements: Accomplishing goals together strengthens your partnership and creates a sense of shared achievement.

Strategies for Planning Fun and Adventurous Activities

Consider His Interests and Comfort Zone

Tailored Activities: Choose activities that align with your husband's interests and comfort level. Consider his likes and dislikes to ensure the experience is enjoyable for both of you.

Gradual Challenges: If he is unfamiliar with adventure, begin with less strenuous activities. As you both get more at ease, gradually up the difficulty level.

Conduct research and make detailed plans in advance: Plan all the essentials, including equipment, safety precautions, and logistics, after doing extensive research on the activity.

Reservations and Permits: To prevent last-minute problems, make any required reservations or permits well in advance.

Safety First Precautions: Put safety first by being aware of the hazards and adopting the necessary safety measures. Wear the appropriate safety gear and abide by the rules.

Emergency Preparedness: Be prepared for emergencies by carrying a first aid kit, knowing the location of the nearest medical facility, and having a plan in place.

Incorporate Variety

Mix It Up: Incorporate a variety of activities to keep things exciting. Alternate between different types of adventures, such as outdoor, water-based, and cultural activities.

New Experiences: Continuously seek out new experiences to explore together. Trying new activities keeps the adventure fresh and exciting.

Fun and Adventurous Activity Ideas

Outdoor Adventures

Hiking and Trekking: Take a walk or trek along picturesque paths and national parks to discover nature. Select hiking routes based on your interests and degree of fitness.

Camping: Arrange a trip where you may spend time in the great outdoors. Savor outdoor activities such as cooking, stargazing, and building a campfire.

Rock Climbing: Put yourself to the test by bouldering or rock climbing.

Water-Related Activities

Canoeing and Kayaking: Take a day to go canoeing or kayaking on the water. Enjoy the view as you paddle across lakes, rivers, or coastal locations.

Snorkelling and Scuba Diving: Take a snorkel or dive to explore the underwater environment. Investigate shipwrecks, coral reefs, and marine life.

White Water Rafting: Take on the exhilaration of river white water rafting. Select a river where the rapids are within your comfort and skill level.

Sexy Activities and Experiments

Skydiving: Take part in skydiving to get the greatest burst of excitement. A fantastic place to start is with tandem jumps with an instructor.

Bungee Jumping: Take a risk by participating in bungee jumping. Leaping from a bridge or platform is an incredible thrill.

Paragliding: Take to the skies and soar through it. Savor the sensation of flying and the amazing views.

Cultural and Urban Adventures

City Exploration: Explore a new city together. Visit landmarks, museums, and local attractions. Try new foods and immerse yourselves in the local culture.

Festivals and Events: Go to sporting events, music festivals, or cultural festivals. These encounters can be enjoyable as well as culturally enlightening.

Escape rooms: Put your cooperation and problem-solving abilities to the test. To solve problems and escape, cooperate with one another.

Do It Yourself Adventures

Backyard Camping: For a comfortable and practical camping experience, set up a tent in your backyard. Experience a starry night without having to leave your house.

Treasure Hunt: Set up a treasure hunt in your neighborhood or house with puzzles and rewards. Spending time together in this engaging and involved manner may be delightful.

Adventure Challenges: Make a list of short trips or tasks that you and your partner can accomplish together, including trying a new dish, picking up a new skill, or finishing a fitness challenge.

Overcoming Barriers to Fun and Adventurous Activities

Busy Schedules

Weekend Adventures: Plan adventures on weekends or days off to accommodate busy work schedules. Short, day-long activities can be just as exciting as longer trips.

Time Management: Improve time management to carve out time for adventure. Prioritize these activities as important parts of your relationship.

Budget Constraints

Affordable Adventures: Choose affordable adventures, such as hiking, biking, or exploring local attractions. Many exciting activities don't require a large budget.

Saving for Adventure: Set aside a small amount of money regularly to fund larger, more expensive adventures. This allows you to plan and save for bigger trips or activities.

Different Comfort Levels

Respect Boundaries: Respect each other's comfort levels and boundaries. Choose activities that both partners are comfortable with and gradually increase the level of challenge.

Open Communication: Communicate openly about your preferences and concerns. Find a balance that ensures both partners enjoy the experience.

Practical Tips for Successful Fun and Adventurous Activities

Stay Positive and Flexible

Positive Attitude: Maintain a positive attitude, even if things don't go as planned. Embrace the adventure and enjoy the experience, regardless of any challenges.

Flexibility: Be flexible with your plans. Sometimes, unexpected changes can lead to new and exciting experiences.

Document the Adventure

Photos and Videos: Capture the moments with photos and videos. Documenting your adventures allows you to relive the memories and share them with others.

Adventure Journal: Keep an adventure journal where you record your experiences, thoughts, and highlights from each activity. This can be a wonderful keepsake.

Reflect and Plan Future Adventures

Reflection: After each adventure, take time to reflect on the experience. Discuss what you enjoyed, what you learned, and what you'd like to do next.

Future Planning: Use your reflections to plan future adventures. Continuously seek out new and exciting activities to keep the sense of adventure alive.

By incorporating fun and adventurous activities into your relationship, you create opportunities for excitement, growth, and deeper connection. These shared experiences not only strengthen your bond but also add joy and variety to your relationship, ensuring that it remains dynamic and fulfilling.

Building Traditions Together

Creating and nurturing traditions together is a powerful way to solidify your bond, create lasting memories, and establish a sense of continuity and stability in your relationship. Traditions can range from simple daily rituals to elaborate annual celebrations. Let's look at the significance of building traditions with your husband and offers detailed ideas and strategies for creating meaningful and enjoyable traditions that can enhance your relationship.

The Importance of Building Traditions

Creates a Sense of Belonging and Stability

Continuity: Traditions provide a sense of continuity and stability in a relationship, offering predictable and comforting rituals.

Belonging: Shared traditions foster a sense of belonging and identity as a couple, reinforcing your connection and commitment.

Strengthens Emotional Bonds

Shared Experiences: Engaging in regular traditions creates shared experiences and memories, which strengthen your emotional bond.

Connection: Traditions offer opportunities for meaningful interaction and connection, deepening your relationship.

Enhances Relationship Satisfaction

Joy and Anticipation: Traditions bring joy and anticipation, contributing to overall relationship satisfaction and happiness.

Celebration and Reflection: Traditions provide moments for celebration and reflection, allowing you to appreciate your journey together.

Promotes Personal and Mutual Growth

Growth and Evolution: Traditions can evolve over time, reflecting your growth and changes as a couple. They can incorporate new interests, experiences, and milestones.

Shared Goals: Creating and maintaining traditions often involves setting and achieving shared goals, promoting teamwork and mutual support.

Strategies for Building Traditions

Identify Shared Interests and Values

Common Ground: Focus on activities and rituals that reflect your shared interests and values. This ensures that the traditions are meaningful and enjoyable for both partners.

Personal Touches: Add your own special twists to the rituals to make them more meaningful and specific to your relationship.

Begin Small and Easy to Transition into Customs: Begin with little, manageable customs that are straightforward to uphold. Because of this, incorporating them into your routine is simpler and you won't feel overwhelmed.

Consistency: The secret is consistency. Whether the custom is weekly, monthly, or yearly, make sure you stick to it consistently.

Be Adaptable and Willing to Change

Adapt and Change: Have the willingness to modify and advance your customs when necessary. Traditions are kept enjoyable and relevant throughout time by being flexible.

Add New Components: Don't be scared to experiment with different activities or add new components to your traditions. This maintains things interesting and novel.

Communicate and Collaborate

Joint Decision-Making: Collaborate with your husband to decide on and plan traditions. Ensure that both partners have a say and feel invested in the rituals.

Open Dialogue: Maintain an open dialogue about your traditions. Discuss what works, what doesn't, and how you can improve or expand them.

Ideas for Building Traditions Together

Daily and Weekly Traditions

Morning Routine: Establish a morning routine that you both enjoy, such as having breakfast together, taking a walk, or sharing a cup of coffee.

Evening Rituals: Create an evening ritual, like reading together, watching a favorite TV show, or sharing highlights of your day.

Weekly Date Night: Set aside one night each week for a date night. This could involve dining out, cooking together, watching a movie, or engaging in a shared hobby.

Seasonal and Annual Traditions

Holiday Celebrations: Develop special ways to celebrate holidays. This could include decorating your home, preparing traditional meals, or visiting family and friends.

Anniversary Rituals: Celebrate your anniversary with a specific tradition, such as revisiting the place where you first met, writing love letters to each other, or planning a getaway.

Seasonal Activities: Engage in seasonal activities, like apple picking in the fall, building snowmen in the winter, hiking in the spring, or having beach days in the summer.

Milestone and Achievement Traditions

Career Milestones: Celebrate career achievements, like promotions or project completions, with a special dinner, a toast, or a small gift.

Personal Goals: Acknowledge personal milestones, such as completing a fitness challenge, learning a new skill, or achieving a personal goal, with a celebratory tradition.

Joint Accomplishments: Celebrate joint accomplishments, such as buying a house, completing a renovation, or reaching a relationship goal, with a meaningful tradition.

Special Occasion Traditions

Birthdays: Develop a unique way to celebrate birthdays. This could include a surprise party, a favorite meal, or a special outing.

Valentine's Day: Create a Valentine's Day tradition, like writing each other heartfelt letters, planning a romantic date, or exchanging thoughtful gifts.

New Year's Eve: Establish a New Year's Eve tradition, such as making resolutions together, hosting a party, or watching fireworks.

Adventure and Travel Traditions

Annual Trips: Plan an annual trip to a destination you both love or want to explore. This could be a weekend getaway, a road trip, or an international vacation.

Local Explorations: Develop a tradition of exploring local attractions, like visiting a new restaurant, museum, or park each month.

Bucket List Activities: Create a bucket list of activities you want to do together and make it a tradition to check off a few items each year.

Overcoming Barriers to Building Traditions

Busy Schedules

Prioritization: Make your traditions a priority by scheduling them in advance and treating them as important commitments.

Flexibility: Be flexible with timing. If you can't stick to a strict schedule, find alternative times to engage in your traditions.

Different Preferences

Compromise: Find a balance between your preferences. Choose activities that both partners enjoy and are willing to participate in.

Alternating Traditions: Alternate between traditions that cater to each partner's interests. This ensures that both partners feel valued and included.

Budget Constraints

Budget-Friendly Options: Opt for budget-friendly traditions that don't require significant financial investment. Simple activities can be just as meaningful and enjoyable.

Saving for Special Traditions: Save up for more elaborate traditions. Setting aside a small amount regularly can help fund special occasions or trips.

Practical Tips for Successful Traditions

Document and Celebrate

Photos and Videos: Capture moments from your traditions with photos and videos. This helps you document and celebrate your shared experiences.

Memory Book: Create a memory book or scrapbook to record your traditions. Include photos, notes, and mementos from each activity.

Reflect and Appreciate

Reflection: Take time to reflect on your traditions and their impact on your relationship. Discuss what you enjoy and how the traditions have strengthened your bond.

Gratitude: Express gratitude for each other and the effort put into maintaining the traditions. Acknowledging the significance of these rituals enhances their meaning.

Continuously Improve

Feedback and Adaptation: Regularly seek feedback from each other and be willing to adapt and improve your traditions. This ensures they remain enjoyable and relevant.

Novel Concepts: Always look for fresh approaches and pastimes to add to your customs. This avoids boredom and keeps things interesting.

Include Friends and Family in Common Traditions: Include your loved ones and friends in a few of your customs. This has the potential to strengthen the bond between people and expand the circle of support.

New Traditions: Establish new customs that involve friends or extended family to promote harmony and delight among all.

Together, you may strengthen your bond, make enduring memories, and cultivate a sense of security and closeness by creating traditions. You may establish traditions that energize and deepen your connection by finding common interests, beginning small, being adaptable, and never stopping learning.

Chapter 5

Deepening Intimacy

Emotional Intimacy

Emotional intimacy A solid and satisfying relationship is built on emotional connection. It entails a strong emotional bond in which both parties experience support, understanding, and value. Emotional closeness must be developed and maintained through work, vulnerability, and respect for one another.

The Value of Emotional Closeness Enhances the Emotional Bond

Connection: Deep emotional connections are fostered by emotional intimacy, which also strengthens partners' sense of oneness and closeness.

Support: It offers a strong base of support so that both partners feel appreciated and understood, which fosters confidence and mutual trust.

Enhances Communication

Openness: Emotional intimacy encourages open and honest communication, allowing partners to share their thoughts, feelings, and concerns freely.

Understanding: It promotes a deeper understanding of each other's emotions, needs, and desires, facilitating effective and empathetic communication.

Promotes Relationship Satisfaction

Fulfillment: Emotional intimacy contributes to overall relationship satisfaction and fulfillment, as both partners feel emotionally connected and appreciated.

Security: It creates a sense of emotional security, reducing feelings of loneliness, anxiety, and insecurity within the relationship.

Builds Resilience

Coping Mechanism: A strong emotional bond provides a robust coping mechanism during challenging times, enabling partners to navigate difficulties together.

Conflict Resolution: Emotional intimacy aids in resolving conflicts constructively, as it fosters empathy, patience, and understanding.

Strategies for Cultivating Emotional Intimacy

Prioritize Quality Time Together

Dedicated Time: Set aside dedicated time to spend together without distractions. Regularly engaging in meaningful activities can strengthen your emotional connection.

Daily Rituals: Establish daily rituals, such as sharing a meal, taking a walk, or having a bedtime conversation, to maintain consistent emotional engagement.

Practice Active Listening

Attention and Presence: Give your full attention when your husband is speaking. Show that you are fully present and engaged in the conversation.

Reflective Listening: Reflect back what your husband is saying to ensure understanding and validate his feelings. This demonstrates empathy and respect.

Share Your Feelings and Thoughts

Vulnerability: Be open and vulnerable in sharing your own feelings and thoughts. This encourages your husband to reciprocate, deepening emotional intimacy.

Express Appreciation: Regularly express appreciation and gratitude for your husband. Acknowledging his efforts and qualities strengthens your emotional bond.

Create a Safe Emotional Space

Non-Judgmental Environment: Foster a non-judgmental and supportive environment where both partners feel safe to express their true selves.

Respect and Empathy: Show respect and empathy for each other's feelings and experiences. Avoid criticism, blame, or dismissive behavior.

Engage in Meaningful Conversations

Deep Topics: Engage in conversations about deep and meaningful topics, such as your dreams, fears, and values. These discussions can foster a deeper emotional connection.

Ask Questions: Ask open-ended questions that encourage thoughtful responses and deeper insights into each other's inner worlds.

Support Each Other's Emotional Needs

Emotional Support: Be there for your husband during emotional highs and lows. Offer comfort, encouragement, and reassurance when needed.

Understanding Needs: Understand and respond to your husband's emotional needs. Be attentive to what makes him feel loved, supported, and appreciated.

Ideas for Building Emotional Intimacy

Regular Date Nights

Scheduled Dates: Schedule regular date nights to focus on each other and nurture your relationship. Choose activities that you both enjoy and that facilitate connection.

Intimate Settings: Opt for intimate settings that encourage meaningful conversations, such as a cozy dinner, a walk in the park, or a quiet evening at home.

Emotional Check-Ins

Weekly Check-Ins: Have weekly emotional check-ins where you discuss your feelings, thoughts, and experiences from the past week. This practice keeps you emotionally aligned.

Honesty and Openness: Be honest and open during these check-ins, sharing both positive and challenging emotions.

Couples Therapy or Workshops

Professional Advice: To strengthen your emotional bond and take care of any underlying difficulties, think about attending workshops or couples' therapy. Expert advice can offer priceless resources and insights.

Building Skills: You can develop critical abilities like empathy, effective communication, and conflict resolution with the aid of these lessons.

Similar Interests and Hobbies

Common Activities: By enjoying and working together, engaging in common interests and hobbies can promote emotional intimacy.

Learning Together: Take a class or begin a new project together to learn something new. Learning together can strengthen your relationship.

Express Physical Affection

Touch and Closeness: Regularly express physical affection, such as hugs, kisses, and holding hands. Physical touch is a powerful way to reinforce emotional connection.

Intimate Moments: Create intimate moments that focus on closeness and affection, such as cuddling while watching a movie or giving each other massages.

Mindfulness and Meditation

Mindful Practices: Practice mindfulness and meditation together to enhance emotional awareness and presence. These practices can reduce stress and increase emotional connection.

Shared Reflection: Reflect together on your experiences with mindfulness and meditation, discussing the insights and feelings that arise.

Overcoming Barriers to Emotional Intimacy

Busy Lifestyles

Prioritize Relationship: Make your relationship a priority by scheduling time for each other despite busy schedules. Consistent effort is key to maintaining emotional intimacy.

Small Moments: Utilize small moments throughout the day to connect emotionally. Even brief, meaningful interactions can make a difference.

Emotional Barriers

Address Issues: Address any emotional barriers or past hurts that may hinder emotional intimacy. Seek professional help if needed to work through these issues.

Open Communication: Foster open communication about emotional barriers and work together to overcome them with empathy and understanding.

Differences in Emotional Expression

Respect Differences: Respect each other's differences Recognize that every person processes and expresses emotions in a different way.

Modification and Sacrifice: To meet the emotional requirements of one another, adjust and make concessions. Strike a balance that benefits both parties.

Useful Advice for Increasing Emotional Closeness

Continue to be persistent and patient:

Maintain consistency in your endeavors to cultivate emotional closeness. It calls for constant work and commitment from both parties.

Patience: Give the procedure your whole attention. Deep emotional connection cannot be rushed; it must be developed over time.

Celebrate Emotional Milestones

Acknowledge Growth: Celebrate emotional milestones, such as overcoming a significant challenge together or achieving a deeper level of understanding.

Positive Reinforcement: Reinforce positive emotional behaviors and efforts with appreciation and encouragement.

Seek Feedback and Improvement

Open Feedback: Encourage open feedback from your husband about your emotional connection and ways to improve it. Constructive feedback fosters growth.

Continuous Improvement: Continuously seek to improve your emotional intimacy through new strategies, activities, and communication techniques.

By prioritizing and nurturing emotional intimacy, you can create a deep and lasting connection with your husband that enhances every aspect of your relationship. Through consistent effort, open communication, and mutual support, you can build a strong emotional bond that stands the test of time.

Physical Intimacy

Physical intimacy is a fundamental aspect of romantic relationships, providing a powerful means of expressing love, affection, and desire. For many men, physical touch and closeness are primary ways of feeling connected and valued in a relationship. Here, we will explore various dimensions of physical intimacy and offer practical tips on how to use it to deepen the romantic bond with your husband.

Understanding Physical Intimacy

Physical intimacy goes beyond just sexual activity; it encompasses all forms of touch and physical closeness that convey affection and emotional connection. This includes holding hands, hugging, kissing, cuddling, and other non-sexual touches. Recognizing the importance of these gestures can help in creating a more profound and fulfilling relationship.

The Significance of Physical Intimacy in a Relationship

Emotional Connection: Developing and strengthening an emotional bond with your spouse can be achieved through physical intimacy. The "love hormone," oxytocin, is released through touch and strengthens bonds and trust.

Communication: Words frequently cannot convey what a physical touch can. A kiss can indicate love, an embrace can show support, and holding hands can symbolize unity and collaboration.

Health Benefits: By lowering blood pressure, strengthening the immune system, and reducing stress, regular physical closeness can enhance general health.

Types of Physical Intimacy

Touch:

Everyday Touches: Simple gestures like touching his arm while talking, playing with his hair, or gently placing your hand on his back can make him feel loved and appreciated.

Affectionate Touches: More deliberate actions like cuddling on the couch, massaging his shoulders, or holding hands while walking can enhance closeness and affection.

Hugging:

Hugs are a universal sign of comfort and support. Embrace your husband often, whether it's to greet him, say goodbye, or just to show you care. Hugs can reduce stress and increase feelings of security and connection.

Kissing:

Pecks and Quick Kisses: These can be used throughout the day to show affection and maintain a connection.

Passionate Kissing: Taking time for more intimate kisses can rekindle passion and enhance romantic feelings.

Sexual Activity:

Consensual Intercourse: Sexual intimacy is a vital part of many romantic relationships. Understanding each other's desires and boundaries is essential for a fulfilling sexual relationship.

Non-Penetrative Activities: Exploring other forms of sexual intimacy, such as oral sex, manual stimulation, or simply lying naked together, can deepen your connection.

Enhancing Physical Intimacy with Your Husband

Open Communication:

Discuss your needs, preferences, and boundaries openly. Encourage your husband to do the same. Understanding each other's desires can help you both feel more satisfied and connected.

Prioritize Intimacy:

Make physical intimacy a priority. Schedule regular date nights, plan romantic getaways, or simply set aside time each day to be close to each other.

Explore New Experiences:

Together, try new things to keep the spark alive. This may include exploring each other's dreams, trying out various forms of contact, or creating a romantic setting with candles and calming music.

Pay Attention and React Correctly:

Observe how your spouse reacts to various types of contact. It demonstrates your concern for his comfort and enjoyment that you pay attention to his requirements and desires.

Establish a Cozy Environment: Make sure your bedroom and house are suitable for closeness. Make sure the area is tidy, cozy, and distraction-free.

Practical Tips for Romancing Your Husband through Physical Intimacy

Surprise Him with Touch:

Initiate unexpected moments of touch throughout the day. A surprise hug, a kiss on the cheek, or a gentle caress can make him feel loved and desired.

Initiate Physical Closeness:

Avoid waiting for him to initiate the first move. Initiate physical contact with him to express your desire; this can be as simple as holding his hand, kissing him passionately, or cuddling up on the sofa.

Use Physical Intimacy to Reduce Stress: Give your spouse a warm hug or a calming massage to help him unwind after a demanding day. Touching him physically can be a very effective approach to reduce tension and demonstrate your concern for his well.

Celebrate Special Occasions: Express your love and affection on important days. Utilize physical closeness to add special touches to any special occasion, be it an anniversary, birthday, or just a momentous occasion.

Don't wait for him to make the first move. Show your desire by initiating physical closeness, whether it's cuddling on the couch, holding his hand, or giving him a passionate kiss.

Use Physical Intimacy to Alleviate Stress:

After a long day, help your husband relax with a soothing massage or a warm hug. Physical touch can be a powerful way to alleviate stress and show that you care about his well-being.

Celebrate Special Moments:

Mark special occasions with intimate gestures. Whether it's a birthday, anniversary, or just a significant moment, use physical intimacy to make the day memorable.

Maintain Physical Intimacy During Conflict:

Physical touch can help de-escalate conflicts and reinforce that you are a team. A simple touch or hug during a disagreement can show that you still care about each other, despite the conflict.

Physical intimacy is a vital part of romancing your husband and maintaining a healthy, happy relationship. By understanding its importance and actively nurturing it, you can deepen your emotional connection, enhance communication, and create a more fulfilling and loving partnership. Remember, the key to successful physical intimacy is mutual respect, open communication, and a willingness to explore and grow together.

Romantic Touches and Gestures

Romantic touches and gestures are powerful tools in expressing love and deepening the emotional connection with your husband. These acts, often simple and spontaneous, can convey affection, appreciation, and desire, making him feel valued and cherished.

Understanding Romantic Touches and Gestures

Romantic touches and gestures go beyond routine physical contact. They are deliberate acts of love that show your husband how much he means to you. These actions can be spontaneous or planned, grand or subtle, but their primary purpose is to strengthen your bond and keep the romance alive.

The Significance of Romantic Touches and Gestures

Emotional Connection:

Romantic gestures help build and maintain an emotional connection. They remind your husband of your love and commitment, reinforcing the bond between you.

Communication:

Actions often speak louder than words. Romantic touches and gestures can convey emotions and sentiments that might be difficult to express verbally.

Keeping the Spark Alive:

Regular romantic gestures prevent the relationship from becoming stagnant. They add excitement and spontaneity, keeping the romance fresh and vibrant.

Types of Romantic Touches

Gentle Caresses:

A soft touch on the face, a gentle stroke of his hair, or a light touch on his arm can be incredibly intimate and reassuring. These small gestures show your affection and care.

Hand-Holding:

Holding hands is a simple yet powerful gesture. Whether you're walking together, sitting side by side, or lying in bed, holding hands can create a sense of unity and connection.

Cuddling:

Cuddling fosters closeness and comfort. Whether you're watching a movie, talking, or just relaxing, cuddling can strengthen your bond and make your husband feel loved and secure.

Kissing:

Forehead Kisses: A kiss on the forehead is a tender and protective gesture, showing your care and affection.

Cheek Kisses: Light kisses on the cheek can be playful and affectionate, adding a touch of sweetness to your interactions.

Passionate Kisses: Deep, passionate kisses can reignite the spark and remind your husband of your romantic and sexual desire for him.

Back Rubs and Massages:

Offering a back rub or massage is a wonderful way to show your husband you care about his well-being. It's a gesture that combines physical touch with relaxation, helping to relieve stress and tension.

Types of Romantic Gestures

Surprise Notes and Messages:

Leave little love notes in places he'll find them, such as his wallet, car, or on the bathroom mirror. Text him sweet messages during the day to let him know you're thinking about him.

Thoughtful Gifts:

Surprise him with small, thoughtful gifts that show you know and appreciate his interests. It doesn't have to be expensive—a book he's been wanting to read, his favorite snack, or a new gadget can show your thoughtfulness.

Acts of Service:

Doing something special for him, like making his favorite meal, taking care of a chore he dislikes, or planning a relaxing evening for him, can be incredibly romantic. These actions show that you pay attention to his needs and want to make his life easier.

Quality Time:

Spending uninterrupted time together doing something you both enjoy can be deeply romantic. Whether it's a walk in the park, a movie night at home, or a weekend getaway, the key is to be fully present and engaged with each other.

Romantic Dates:

Plan special dates that cater to his interests and create memorable experiences. It could be a picnic under the stars, a visit to a place he loves, or a surprise dinner at a fancy restaurant.

Compliments and Affirmations:

Regularly compliment your husband and affirm your love and appreciation for him. Tell him what you admire about him, praise his efforts, and express your gratitude for having him in your life.

Practical Tips for Implementing Romantic Touches and Gestures

Be Attentive and Observant:

Pay attention to your husband's reactions to different gestures. Notice what makes him smile, relax, or feel appreciated, and incorporate more of those actions into your routine.

Be Genuine:

Ensure that your gestures and touches are sincere. Authenticity is crucial in making your husband feel genuinely loved and appreciated.

Balance Spontaneity and Planning:

While spontaneous gestures are often the most memorable, planning special moments can also add excitement and anticipation. Find a balance between the two to keep the romance dynamic.

Personalize Your Gestures:

Tailor your romantic touches and gestures to your husband's preferences and personality. What works for one person might not work for another, so it's important to know what makes your husband feel special.

Express Gratitude:

Regularly thank your husband for his love, support, and the things he does for you. Gratitude reinforces positive behavior and strengthens your bond.

Romantic touches and gestures are essential components of a loving and fulfilling relationship. By incorporating these actions into your daily life, you can keep the romance alive, strengthen your emotional connection, and make your husband feel cherished and valued. Remember, it's the thought and effort behind these gestures that matter the most, so be creative, be sincere, and most importantly, be loving.

Keeping the Passion Alive

Maintaining passion in a long-term relationship requires effort, creativity, and dedication. It's easy for daily routines and responsibilities to overshadow romantic and passionate moments, but keeping the spark alive is essential for a fulfilling and enduring marriage.

Understanding Passion in a Relationship

Passion is characterized by intense emotions, enthusiasm, and strong affection. It encompasses both physical and emotional intimacy, creating a dynamic and deeply satisfying connection. Over time, the initial intensity of passion may naturally wane, but with intentional actions, you can continually rekindle and sustain it.

The Importance of Keeping Passion Alive

Emotional Fulfillment:

Passionate relationships are often more emotionally satisfying, providing a deeper sense of connection and happiness.

Relationship Satisfaction:

Maintaining passion contributes to overall relationship satisfaction, reducing feelings of monotony and enhancing the quality of your partnership.

Physical and Mental Health:

Passionate intimacy releases endorphins and oxytocin, reducing stress and promoting physical and mental well-being.

Strategies for Keeping the Passion Alive

Prioritize Quality Time Together:

Regular Date Nights: Schedule regular date nights to spend quality time together. Try new activities, explore new places, or revisit favorite spots to keep things exciting.

Weekend Getaways: Plan occasional weekend getaways to break the routine and create memorable experiences together. A change of scenery can reignite passion and provide a fresh perspective on your relationship.

Communicate Openly and Honestly:

Express Desires and Fantasies: Share your desires, fantasies, and what you enjoy in your intimate moments. Open communication about sexual preferences can lead to a more fulfilling and passionate relationship.

Address Issues Promptly: Don't let misunderstandings or conflicts fester. Addressing issues promptly and respectfully helps maintain emotional intimacy and prevents resentment from building.

Keep the Romance Alive:

Surprise Gestures: Surprise your husband with thoughtful gestures, such as leaving love notes, planning a surprise date, or giving him a small gift that shows you're thinking about him.

Acts of Kindness: Small acts of kindness, like making his favorite breakfast or taking care of a task he dislikes, can show your love and appreciation, keeping the romance alive.

Maintain Physical Intimacy:

Touch and Affection: Regular physical touch, such as holding hands, hugging, and cuddling, helps maintain a sense of closeness and affection.

Explore New Intimacy: Try new things in the bedroom to keep your physical relationship exciting. This could include new positions, role-playing, or incorporating sensual activities like massage.

Invest in Personal Growth:

Pursue Individual Interests: Encourage each other to pursue individual hobbies and interests. Personal growth can bring new energy into the relationship and prevent feelings of stagnation.

Set Personal Goals: Working towards personal goals, whether career-related, fitness, or hobbies, can boost self-confidence and contribute positively to your relationship.

Stay Playful and Adventurous:

Play Together: Engage in playful activities together, such as games, sports, or spontaneous adventures. Playfulness can reignite the joy and excitement in your relationship.

Try New Experiences: Explore new hobbies, travel destinations, or activities together. Trying new things can keep your relationship dynamic and exciting.

Show Appreciation and Gratitude:

Express Gratitude: Let your spouse know how much you appreciate all that he does for you on a regular basis. Your relationship is strengthened and excellent behavior is reinforced when you recognize and value one other's efforts.

Honor Achievements: Honor each other's accomplishments, no matter how modest. Sharing joy and a sense of collaboration are fostered when people celebrate triumphs together.

Keep Your Emotional Connectivity:

Deep Talks: Engage in significant, in-depth discussions that transcend everyday routines. Talk about your hopes, worries, and dreams to keep the emotional bond strong.

Empathy and Support: Be there for people when they need it most. Intimacy and trust are strengthened when partners support one another emotionally.

Practical Tips for Sustaining Passion

Schedule Intimate Time:

Life can get busy, and intimacy can sometimes take a back seat. Schedule intimate time to ensure you both prioritize your physical connection.

Create a Romantic Atmosphere:

Set the mood for romance with candles, soft music, and a clean, inviting space. A romantic atmosphere can enhance intimate moments and make them more memorable.

Flirt with Each Other:

Keep the flirtation alive by sending playful texts, giving compliments, and showing affection in small, spontaneous ways.

Reflect on Positive Memories:

Reminisce about happy moments in your relationship. Reflecting on positive memories can rekindle feelings of love and passion.

Stay Physically Active:

Engage in physical activities together, such as dancing, hiking, or working out. Physical activity can boost energy levels and enhance your physical and emotional connection.

Keeping the passion alive in your relationship requires effort, creativity, and a willingness to continually invest in your partnership. By prioritizing quality time, maintaining open communication, staying physically and emotionally connected, and showing appreciation and gratitude, you can sustain a passionate and fulfilling relationship with your husband. Remember, the key to lasting passion is to keep evolving together, embracing new experiences, and cherishing each other every day.

Chapter 6

Navigating Life's Challenges
Supporting Each Other Through Tough Times

Every relationship faces challenges, whether they arise from external pressures or internal conflicts. How couples navigate these tough times can significantly impact the strength and resilience of their bond. Providing unwavering support to your husband during difficult moments is crucial for maintaining a healthy and loving relationship. This chapter explores strategies and practices for effectively supporting each other through life's ups and downs.

Understanding the Importance of Support

Support in a relationship is multifaceted, encompassing emotional, physical, and practical aspects. Being there for your husband during tough times fosters trust, deepens emotional intimacy, and reinforces your commitment to each other. It involves listening, empathizing, and taking actionable steps to alleviate stress and provide comfort.

The Role of Emotional Support

Active Listening:

Be Present: Pay close attention to whatever your husband says. Put electronics like laptops and phones away so you can concentrate on him.

Approve His Emotions: Even if you don't completely comprehend his feelings, acknowledge and affirm them anyway. Expressing empathy and comprehension by saying something like, "I can see why you feel that way,"

Motivation and Comfort:

Offer Words of Encouragement: Remind him of his qualities and abilities and offer encouraging remarks. Sayings like "I believe in you" or "You're doing great" can help him feel more confident.

Be Reassuring: Reassure him that you're in this together. Let him know that you'll support him no matter what and that you believe in your partnership.

Emotional Availability:

Be Emotionally Present: Be available to discuss his concerns and feelings. Show empathy and offer comfort without judgment.

Express Your Emotions: Share your own feelings and experiences to create a safe space for open emotional exchange.

Practical Support Strategies

Shared Responsibilities:

Divide Tasks Equally: Share household responsibilities and ensure that both partners contribute equally. This reduces stress and prevents one person from feeling overwhelmed.

Step Up When Needed: During particularly tough times, take on more responsibilities to lighten his load. Whether it's managing household chores, childcare, or work-related tasks, your support can make a significant difference.

Problem-Solving Together:

Work together on Solutions: Come up with solutions to problems as a team. As a team, evaluate choices, balance benefits and drawbacks, and reach conclusions.

Embrace Compromise: Be prepared to give in and look for a middle ground. The secret to solving problems effectively is to be flexible and understanding.

Bringing Comfort to the Body:

Physical Touch: Hugs, handshakes, and light touches can occasionally be incredibly relieving and comforting.

Establish a Calm Environment: Turn your house into a haven for him to rest and recuperate. Stress can be lessened by having a neat, relaxing, and cozy environment.

Supporting Your Husband During Specific Tough Times

Work-Related Stress:

Listen Without Judgment: Allow him to vent about work-related issues without offering immediate solutions. Sometimes, just listening is enough.

Encourage Downtime: Encourage him to take breaks and engage in activities he enjoys to decompress and recharge.

Health Challenges:

Be Informed: Educate yourself about his health condition to better understand what he's going through and how you can help.

Offer Practical Help: Assist with doctor's appointments, medication schedules, and daily tasks. Your practical support can alleviate his stress and allow him to focus on recovery.

Financial Difficulties:

Communicate Openly: Discuss financial concerns openly and honestly. Transparency is crucial in managing financial stress.

Plan Together: Create a budget and financial plan together. Working as a team can help you both feel more in control and less anxious.

Emotional or Mental Health Issues:

Be Patient and Understanding: Mental health issues can be complex and challenging. Show patience, understanding, and compassion.

Encourage Professional Help: Encourage him to seek professional help if needed. Offer to accompany him to appointments or support him in finding the right resources.

Maintaining Your Own Well-Being

Supporting your husband through tough times is essential, but it's equally important to take care of your own well-being. A healthy and balanced individual is better equipped to provide support.

Self-Care Practices:

Prioritize Your Health: Maintain a healthy lifestyle through regular exercise, balanced nutrition, and adequate sleep.

Find Time for Yourself: Engage in activities that bring you joy and relaxation. Whether it's a hobby, reading, or spending time with friends, ensure you have time for yourself.

Seek Support:

Reach Out to Loved Ones: Don't hesitate to seek support from friends, family, or a therapist. Having a support system can provide you with the emotional strength needed to support your husband.

Share duties: Don't do every duty by yourself. Assign duties and request assistance as need.

Useful Advice for Encouragement of Continual Check-Ins:

Plan frequent check-ins to talk about how you're both feeling and what kind of assistance you might require from one another. Being open with one another facilitates understanding and timely resolution of issues.

Establish Rituals of Attachment: Create routines that strengthen your relationship, like a weekly date night, a morning coffee ritual, or an evening stroll. These customs offer dependable chances for assistance and connection.

Practice Gratitude:

Express gratitude for each other regularly. Acknowledging and appreciating each other's efforts fosters a positive environment and reinforces your commitment.

Stay Flexible:

Be adaptable and willing to adjust your support as needed. Tough times can be unpredictable, and flexibility ensures you're both responsive to each other's changing needs.

Supporting each other through tough times is a cornerstone of a strong and loving relationship. By providing emotional, practical, and physical support, you reinforce your bond and demonstrate your commitment to each other's well-being. Remember, maintaining open communication, showing empathy, and practicing self-care are essential components of effective support. Together, you can navigate life's challenges and emerge stronger as a couple, continually deepening your love and partnership.

Balancing Work, Family, and Romance

In today's fast-paced world, finding a balance between work, family responsibilities, and maintaining a romantic relationship can be challenging. However, striking this balance is crucial for a harmonious and fulfilling life. Here we delve into strategies and insights to help you manage these demands while keeping the romance alive in your marriage.

Understanding the Challenges

Balancing work, family, and romance involves managing multiple roles and responsibilities. Each aspect demands time, energy, and attention, and neglecting any one area can lead to stress and dissatisfaction. Recognizing the challenges is the first step towards finding effective solutions.

The Importance of Balance

Maintaining Relationship Health:

A balanced life ensures that your relationship doesn't take a backseat. Investing time and effort in your marriage strengthens your bond and keeps the romance alive.

Reducing Stress:

Balancing work and family responsibilities with romance can reduce stress and prevent burnout. It allows you to enjoy each aspect of your life without feeling overwhelmed.

Enhancing Quality of Life:

Achieving balance enhances your overall quality of life, making you feel more fulfilled and content.

Strategies for Balancing Work, Family, and Romance

Prioritize and Plan:

Set Priorities: Identify what's most important to you and your husband. Prioritize tasks and activities that align with your values and goals.

Create a Schedule: Develop a weekly schedule that allocates time for work, family, and romance. Planning helps ensure that you dedicate time to each area without neglecting any.

Effective Time Management:

Set Boundaries: Establish Boundaries: Draw distinct lines separating work and personal time. Do not check emails or bring work home during family time. Make Good Use of Your Time: Take advantage of quiet times and transitional spaces. For instance, talk about your day or listen to an audiobook together throughout your commute.

Talk Honestly:

Frequent Check-Ins: Talk about schedules, duties, and any necessary adjustments with your spouse at regular check-ins. Managing expectations and minimizing confrontations are made easier with open communication.

Communicate Your Needs and Fears: Talk to your husband about your needs and worries. Talk about any difficulties you're having juggling work, family, and romance, then collaborate to find answers.

Share Responsibilities:

Divide Tasks Equally: Ensure that household and family responsibilities are shared equally. This prevents one person from feeling overwhelmed and allows both partners to have time for romance.

Support Each Other: Offer support during busy or stressful periods. For example, if your husband has a demanding work project, take on more household responsibilities and vice versa.

Create Quality Family Time:

Family Activities: Plan regular family activities that everyone enjoys. This strengthens family bonds and provides opportunities for fun and relaxation.

Include Romantic Moments: Integrate romantic moments into family time. For example, cook a meal together as a family and then enjoy a quiet dinner with your husband after the kids are asleep.

Maintain Personal Well-Being:

Self-Care: Prioritize self-care in order to keep your physical and mental health in check. To manage stress and maintain energy, it's imperative to practice regular exercise, consume a good diet, and get enough sleep.

Personal Interests: Follow your passions and interests. Having a happy personal life makes it easier for you to make a good contribution to your partnership.

Helpful Advice for Juggling Work, Family, and Romance

Plan Date Nights: To spend quality time with your partner, schedule frequent date nights. Date nights, whether they're spent at home or on the town, keep your love relationship strong.

Leverage Technology:

Use technology to stay connected throughout the day. Send sweet texts, share updates, or schedule video calls during breaks to keep the romance alive.

Delegate Tasks:

Don't hesitate to delegate tasks to other family members or hire help if needed. Delegating tasks frees up time for you to focus on your relationship.

Be Present:

Practice mindfulness and be present in the moment. Whether you're at work, with family, or spending time with your husband, being fully engaged enhances the quality of your interactions.

Celebrate Milestones:

Celebrate personal and professional milestones together. Acknowledge achievements and special occasions, and use these moments to strengthen your bond.

Overcoming Common Obstacles

Work Stress:

Solution: Develop healthy coping mechanisms for work stress, such as exercise, meditation, or hobbies. Communicate with your husband about your stressors and seek his support.

Lack of Time:

Solution: Reevaluate your schedule and prioritize tasks. Focus on quality rather than quantity when it comes to time spent with family and your husband.

Disagreements on Priorities:

Solution: Discuss your priorities and objectives in an open and honest manner. Find a middle ground that works for both parties and make a compromise.

Demands for Childcare:

Solution: Make plans to have friends, family, or professional services help with childcare. To guarantee that your relationship stays a top priority, schedule frequent couple time.

Balancing work, family, and romance is an ongoing process that requires effort, communication, and flexibility. By setting priorities, managing time effectively, and supporting each other, you can create a harmonious and fulfilling life. Remember, the key to maintaining balance is to stay connected, be present, and continually nurture your relationship. With dedication and intentional actions, you can successfully manage your various roles and responsibilities while keeping the romance alive in your marriage.

Coping with Stress and Fatigue

Stress and fatigue are common challenges in modern life, often stemming from demanding work schedules, family responsibilities, and daily pressures. These factors can take a toll on your physical health, mental well-being, and romantic relationship. Strategies to manage stress and fatigue, ensuring you and your husband can maintain a loving and supportive relationship even during the most trying times are provided here.

Understanding Stress and Fatigue

Stress is the body's response to any demand or threat, while fatigue is a feeling of constant tiredness or weakness. Both can affect your emotional state, energy levels, and interactions with your partner. Recognizing the signs and sources of stress and fatigue is the first step in addressing them.

The Impact of Stress and Fatigue on Relationships

Decreased Intimacy:

Stress and fatigue can reduce physical and emotional intimacy. You might feel too exhausted for romantic gestures, affecting your connection.

Increased Irritability:

When you're stressed or tired, you're more likely to be irritable and less patient, leading to conflicts and misunderstandings.

Communication Breakdown:

Stress can hinder effective communication, making it difficult to express your feelings or listen to your partner, causing emotional distance.

Neglecting Quality Time:

Fatigue can make it challenging to spend quality time together, further straining the relationship.

Strategies for Coping with Stress and Fatigue

Effective Stress Management:

Identify Stressors: Recognize the sources of your stress. Whether it's work, financial pressures, or family responsibilities, identifying the root cause can help you address it more effectively.

Develop Healthy Coping Mechanisms: Engage in activities that help you relax and unwind, such as exercise, meditation, or hobbies. Regularly practicing these activities can reduce stress levels.

Prioritize Self-Care:

Physical well-being: Adopt a healthy lifestyle that includes frequent exercise, a balanced diet, and enough sleep. Being in good physical health makes it easier to handle stress and lessens weariness.

Mental Health: Give yourself some time to unwind and rejuvenate. Engaging in hobbies, walks, or reading are all good ways to take care of your mental health.

Effective Time Management:

Establish boundaries: To keep work from invading your personal life, establish distinct boundaries between work and leisure time. Make sure you get some downtime and quality time with your spouse.

Set Task Priorities: Give your whole attention to the most crucial tasks, assigning or delaying the less important ones. Setting priorities eases stress and aids with workload management.

Support Each Other:

Open Communication: Discuss your stress and fatigue with your husband. Sharing your feelings can provide relief and help you both understand each other's challenges.

Offer Practical Support: Assist each other with tasks and responsibilities. Simple acts like sharing household chores or taking care of the kids can alleviate stress and provide more time for relaxation.

Maintain Emotional Connection:

Quality Time: Schedule regular quality time together, even if it's just a short walk or a quiet evening at home. Consistent connection helps maintain intimacy and support.

Affectionate Gestures: Small acts of affection, like holding hands, hugging, or leaving love notes, can reinforce your emotional bond and provide comfort during stressful times.

Professional Help:

Counseling: If stress and fatigue are overwhelming, consider seeking professional counseling or therapy. A therapist can provide strategies to manage stress and improve your mental health.

Medical Advice: Medical Advice: If your exhaustion is getting worse, see a doctor. It can indicate a medical condition that requires further care.

Useful Advice for Controlling Stress and Tiredness Establish a Calm Environment:

Make sure your house is a comfortable and relaxing location. To create a tranquil ambiance, clear the space, diffuse soothing aromas, and turn on relaxing music. Practice Mindfulness: Take part in mindfulness techniques such as meditation or slow, deep breathing. Remaining present and lowering anxiety are two benefits of mindfulness.

Stay Connected with Loved Ones:

Maintain connections with friends and family. Social support is vital for managing stress and improving your overall well-being.

Establish a Routine:

Create a daily routine that includes time for work, family, self-care, and relaxation. A balanced routine helps manage stress and prevents burnout.

Engage in Physical Activity:

Frequent exercise is an effective way to reduce stress and increase energy. Whether it's dancing, yoga, or walking, choose an activity you enjoy doing and include it into your daily routine.

Exercise Gratitude: Pay attention to the positive facets of your relationship and life. Gratitude exercises help you change your perspective and lessen the effects of stress.

Sustaining Romance in the Face of Stress

Arrange Easy Romantic Motions:

Little things like a spontaneous embrace, a favorite dish, or a surprise letter can maintain the romance.

Be Patient and Understanding: Acknowledge that your spouse may also be impacted by stress and exhaustion. Give understanding instead of criticism; be patient and encouraging.

Maintain Open Lines of Communication: Share your feelings regularly. Open communication helps in navigating stressful periods together.

Celebrate Small Wins:

Acknowledge and celebrate small accomplishments and milestones, whether personal or professional. Celebrations provide a positive boost and reinforce your partnership.

Prioritize Intimacy:

Make time for physical intimacy, even if it's just cuddling or holding hands. Physical closeness can reduce stress and strengthen your bond.

Coping with stress and fatigue requires a combination of self-care, effective time management, and mutual support. By prioritizing your well-being, maintaining open communication, and making time for each other, you can navigate challenging times without sacrificing the romance in your relationship. Remember, it's the small, consistent efforts that make a big difference. Together, you and your husband can build a resilient, loving partnership that thrives even in the face of stress and fatigue.

Maintaining Romance in Different Life Stages

Romantic relationships evolve over time, influenced by various life stages and experiences. Each phase brings unique challenges and opportunities for growth, requiring couples to adapt and find new ways to maintain their romantic connection.

The Newlywed Phase

The newlywed phase is often characterized by intense passion and excitement. This is a time of discovery and deepening intimacy as you build the foundation of your life together.

Fostering Emotional Intimacy:

Open Communication: Establish open and honest communication habits. Share your dreams, fears, and expectations to build a strong emotional connection.

Shared Goals: Set goals together, such as planning trips or discussing future aspirations. Working towards common objectives strengthens your partnership.

Keeping the Spark Alive:

Surprise Gestures: Keep the excitement alive with spontaneous romantic gestures, like surprise dates, love notes, or small gifts.

Quality Time: Prioritize spending quality time together, free from distractions. Whether it's a weekend getaway or a simple walk in the park, make time to connect.

Building Traditions:

Create Rituals: Establish traditions, such as weekly date nights or annual trips, that become cherished parts of your relationship.

The Parenting Years

Raising children can bring immense joy but also significant stress and demands on your time and energy. Maintaining romance during this stage requires creativity and intentional effort.

Prioritizing Your Relationship:

Regular Date Nights: Plan frequent date dates to rekindle your relationship and spend quality time together without the kids. A few hours can have a significant impact. Every Day Check-Ins: Establish a routine of checking in every day to discuss your thoughts and feelings. This maintains open channels of communication.

Sharing Responsibilities:

Teamwork: Assist one another in handling parenting and home duties. By splitting the workload, couples may relax and spend more time together.

Encourage One Another: Show each other compassion and empathy for one another's struggles and requirements. When you can, assist and encourage others.

Finding Moments of Intimacy:

Small Gestures: Show affection through small gestures like a hug, a kiss, or a loving note. These moments can maintain a sense of closeness.

Intimacy Rituals: Establish intimacy rituals, such as cuddling before bed or having a quiet morning coffee together, to nurture your connection.

The Empty Nest

When children grow up and leave home, couples often find themselves with more time to focus on each other. This can be a period of rediscovery and renewed romance.

Rediscover Each Other:

Explore New Interests: Take up new hobbies or activities together that you both enjoy. This can reignite your sense of adventure and curiosity.

Travel Together: Plan trips to places you've always wanted to visit. Traveling together provides opportunities for shared experiences and bonding.

Rekindle Romance:

Date Like You Used To: Recreate your early dating experiences. Go to your favorite spots, have fun outings, and relive special moments.

Physical Intimacy: With more privacy, focus on enhancing your physical intimacy. Take time to explore each other's desires and deepen your physical connection.

Support Personal Growth:

Individual Pursuits: Encourage each other to pursue personal interests and goals. Supporting each other's growth can strengthen your relationship.

Celebrate Achievements: Acknowledge and celebrate each other's accomplishments, no matter how small. This fosters mutual respect and admiration.

Retirement

Retirement brings a significant lifestyle change, often with more free time and opportunities for shared activities. It's a time to focus on your relationship and enjoy the fruits of your labor.

Stay Active Together:

Physical Activities: Engage in physical activities together, such as walking, yoga, or dancing. Staying active promotes health and provides quality time together.

Social Engagement: Participate in social events and community activities. Shared social interactions can enrich your relationship.

Create New Traditions:

Regular Outings: Establish new traditions like weekly outings, hobby clubs, or volunteering together. These activities add structure and enjoyment to your days.

Home Projects: Collaborate on home improvement or gardening projects. Working together on these projects can be fulfilling and strengthen your bond.

Focus on Well-Being:

Health and Wellness: Health and Wellness: Keep a healthy lifestyle as a top priority for your health and wellbeing. Encourage one another to maintain a healthy lifestyle. Be the emotional support system for one another, offering consolation and encouragement while you deal with the difficulties and changes that come with getting older.

Overarching Advice for Preserving Romance at Any Stage

Communication: Throughout all phases of life, keep lines of communication open, sincere, and polite. Having regular conversations about your needs, wants, and expectations improves communication between you and helps to avoid misunderstandings.

Quality Time:

Regardless of life stage, prioritize quality time together. Consistent, meaningful interactions keep the romance alive and ensure you stay connected.

Affection:

Show affection daily, through both words and actions. Small gestures of love and appreciation go a long way in maintaining a strong emotional connection.

Flexibility:

Be flexible and willing to adapt to changes. Life stages bring new challenges and opportunities, and being open to adjusting your approach keeps your relationship dynamic and resilient.

Celebrate Milestones:

Celebrate relationship milestones, such as anniversaries and special occasions. Acknowledging and commemorating these moments reinforces your commitment and love.

Shared Goals:

Set and work towards shared goals, whether they are related to family, career, or personal growth. Achieving these goals together strengthens your partnership and sense of accomplishment.

Maintaining romance through different life stages requires effort, adaptability, and a deep commitment to your partner. By recognizing the unique challenges and opportunities each stage presents, you can find ways to keep the spark alive and nurture your relationship. Remember, the key to enduring romance is continuous growth, open communication, and a shared commitment to making each stage of life together as fulfilling and joyful as possible.

Chapter 7

Growing Together

Personal Development and Growth

Personal development and growth are essential components of a fulfilling and balanced life. When both partners in a marriage commit to their individual growth, it not only enhances their personal well-being but also strengthens their relationship.

Understanding Personal Development and Growth

Activities that increase self-awareness, nurture potential and talents, improve quality of life, and help realize goals and objectives are all considered to be part of personal development. Emotional, intellectual, physical, and spiritual growth are all possible. When a couple makes time for their personal growth, they both bring their best selves to the relationship, which cultivates respect, appreciation, and support for one another.

The Importance of Personal Development in a Relationship

Enhanced Self-Awareness:

Understanding your needs, desires, strengths, and shortcomings is made easier by personal growth, which heightens self-awareness. This self-awareness promotes improved dialogue and lessens miscommunication.

Increased Confidence:

Pursuing personal goals and achieving growth boosts self-confidence. A confident partner is more likely to contribute positively to the relationship, taking initiative and handling challenges effectively.

Better Stress Management:

Developing coping strategies and resilience through personal growth helps manage stress. Reduced stress levels lead to a more harmonious and supportive relationship.

Mutual Respect and Admiration:

Witnessing each other's growth and achievements fosters mutual respect and admiration. Celebrating each other's progress strengthens your emotional connection.

Fulfillment and Happiness:

Personal fulfillment and happiness from pursuing individual passions and goals contribute to overall relationship satisfaction. Happy individuals create a positive and nurturing environment for their partner.

Strategies for Personal Development and Growth

Set Personal Goals:

Identify Aspirations: Reflect on your passions, interests, and long-term dreams. Identify what you want to achieve in different areas of your life, such as career, health, hobbies, or spirituality.

Create a Plan: Develop a clear action plan with specific, measurable, achievable, relevant, and time-bound (SMART) goals. Divide more ambitious objectives into more doable steps.

Accept Lifelong Education:

Go After Education: Participate in workshops, certification programs, or courses to advance your knowledge and abilities. Constant learning creates fresh opportunities and keeps your mind active.

Read Frequently: Develop the habit of reading. Examine periodicals, books, and articles about subjects you are interested in. Reading extends your horizons and fosters intellectual development.

Acquire New Proficiencies:

Pick Up a Hobby: Learn a new skill or pastime, like painting, cooking, gardening, or playing an instrument. Taking part in artistic endeavors enhances mental and emotional health.

Enhance Professional Skills: Put your attention on learning things that will help you in your career. Participate in industry conferences, establish professional connections, or look for a mentor.

Put Your Health First:

Exercise Frequently: Make physical activity a regular part of your schedule. Exercise boosts brain clarity, lowers stress levels, and benefits physical health as well.

Keep Your Diet Balanced: Consume a healthy diet that gives your body and mind energy. A healthy diet promotes vitality and general well-being.

Maintain Your Mental and Emotional Health: Practice mindfulness and meditation to improve your self-awareness and lower your stress levels. These exercises assist you in maintaining your center and awareness.

Therapy and Counselling: To address emotional difficulties, enhance self-awareness, and create healthy coping strategies, think about pursuing therapy or counselling.

Develop Social Networks and Relationships: Create a Network of Support: Develop deep connections with your family, friends, and coworkers. Encouragement and perspective are provided by a robust support system.

Give Back and Volunteer: Take part in volunteer work or community service. Giving back to the community creates a sense of fulfilment and purpose.

Spiritual Growth:

Explore Spiritual Practices: Engage in spiritual practices that resonate with you, such as prayer, meditation, yoga, or attending religious services. Spiritual growth enhances inner peace and resilience.

Supporting Each Other's Growth

Encourage and Celebrate:

Show Interest: Take an active interest in your husband's goals and pursuits. Ask about his progress, offer encouragement, and celebrate his achievements.

Be a Cheerleader: Provide positive reinforcement and support during challenging times. Your belief in his abilities boosts his confidence and motivation.

Create a Growth-Friendly Environment:

Allocate Time: Ensure that both of you have dedicated time for personal pursuits. This might involve adjusting schedules or sharing responsibilities to free up time for growth activities.

Respect Boundaries: Respect each other's need for personal space and time. Encourage independence while maintaining connection.

Engage in Joint Growth Activities:

Learn Together: Enroll in a workshop or class jointly to learn together. Experiences in shared learning can strengthen your relationship and give you conversation points in common.

Establish shared objectives: Establish cooperative objectives, such trip schedules, fitness challenges, or financial benchmarks. As a team, you will improve your cooperation by achieving these goals.

Talk Honestly:

Discuss Aspirations: Have regular conversations about your personal and collective goals. In your personal development travels, open communication promotes understanding and alignment.

Give Constructive Feedback: Encourage one another's development and provide constructive criticism. Be considerate when receiving feedback and concentrate on providing encouragement.

Balance Your Needs in Personal and Relationships: Maintain Contact: Make sure you stay close to each other both physically and emotionally when you work on yourself. Take into account both your personal and your relationship's needs.

Adjust as Needed: As circumstances and priorities change in life, make necessary adjustments. Be adaptable and ready to modify your growth strategies to meet each other's changing requirements.

Useful Advice for Maintaining Personal Development Remain Inspired:

Reviewing your objectives and advancement on a regular basis will help you stay motivated. Remind yourself of the advantages of reaching your goals to keep yourself motivated.

Track Your development: You can use digital tools or keep a journal to keep track of your development. Keeping a journal of your trip helps you identify areas for growth and gives you a sense of success.

Seek Accountability

Look for someone to hold you accountable, a mentor, a buddy, or your spouse. You can stay on course by checking in with someone who encourages your improvement on a regular basis.

Embrace Challenges:

View challenges as opportunities for growth. Embrace setbacks as learning experiences and stay resilient in the face of obstacles.

Celebrate Milestones:

Celebrate your milestones, no matter how small. Acknowledging your achievements boosts your confidence and reinforces your commitment to growth.

Personal development and growth are vital for individual fulfillment and a thriving relationship. By committing to your own growth and supporting your husband's journey, you create a dynamic and resilient partnership. Remember, personal growth is a continuous process that requires dedication, effort, and mutual support. Together, you and your husband can navigate the path of self-improvement, enriching your lives and deepening your love along the way.

Encouraging His Passions and Hobbies

Encouraging your husband's passions and hobbies is not only a gesture of support but also a way to strengthen your relationship by fostering personal growth and happiness.

Understanding the Importance of Encouragement

Personal Fulfillment:

Pursuing passions and hobbies provides intrinsic satisfaction and fulfillment. It allows your husband to explore his interests, relax, and recharge.

Stress Relief:

Engaging in enjoyable activities can reduce stress and promote mental well-being. It serves as a healthy outlet for managing everyday pressures.

Identity and Self-Expression:

Hobbies and passions contribute to your husband's sense of identity and self-expression. They allow him to showcase his talents, creativity, and unique strengths.

Relationship Enrichment:

Supporting your husband's interests strengthens your bond. It demonstrates your care, respect, and commitment to his happiness and personal growth.

Practical Strategies for Encouraging His Passions and Hobbies

Express Interest and Support:

Active Listening: Pay close attention to your spouse when he discusses his interests or pastimes. To find out more, be genuinely curious and pose inquiries.

Give constant Encouragement: Give him vocal encouragement and thanks for all of his hard work and accomplishments. Your encouragement gives him more self-assurance and drive.

Give Time and Resources Away:

Set His Activities First: Acknowledge that he needs time set aside specifically for his activities. Organize timetables to suit his interests and give him undisturbed time. Financial Assistance: Assign funds from the budget for any necessary purchases of gear, lessons, or memberships in associations with his interests. Putting money into his hobbies shows that you care about his well-being.

Engage and Exchange Interests:

Accompany Him: When you can, take part in his interests or activities. You two spend precious time together and your bond is strengthened by this shared experience.

Share Common Interests: Explore mutual interests or discover new hobbies together. Finding activities, you both enjoy fosters camaraderie and strengthens your relationship.

Create a Supportive Environment:

Designated Space: Allocate a dedicated space at home for his hobbies, whether it's a workshop, studio, or quiet corner. This shows respect for his interests and provides a supportive environment.

Remove Barriers: Remove obstacles that hinder his participation in hobbies, such as childcare responsibilities or household chores. Share responsibilities to free up his time.

Celebrate His Achievements:

Acknowledge Milestones: Celebrate his milestones and achievements in his hobbies. Recognize his dedication and effort, and express pride in his accomplishments.

Mark Special Occasions: Consider thoughtful gestures, such as gifts related to his hobbies or planning surprise outings that align with his interests.

Encourage Personal Growth:

Set Goals: Encourage him to set goals and aspirations related to his hobbies. Support his journey towards improvement and mastery.

Provide Feedback: Offer constructive feedback and encouragement to help him refine his skills and achieve his objectives. Your support fuels his passion and commitment.

Benefits of Encouraging His Passions and Hobbies

Strengthened Emotional Connection:

By nurturing his interests, you deepen your emotional bond. Your support demonstrates understanding, empathy, and a willingness to invest in his happiness.

Enhanced Communication:

Discussing hobbies promotes meaningful conversations and strengthens communication. It provides shared topics of interest and fosters a deeper understanding of each other.

Improved Relationship Satisfaction:

Supporting each other's personal growth contributes to overall relationship satisfaction. It creates a partnership based on mutual respect, support, and shared happiness.

Balanced Priorities:

Balancing individual hobbies with shared activities promotes a healthy relationship dynamic. It ensures both partners have space for personal fulfillment while nurturing the relationship.

Overcoming Challenges

Time Constraints:

Prioritize and schedule dedicated time for his hobbies. Coordinate schedules to minimize conflicts and ensure he has uninterrupted time.

Financial Considerations:

Budget accordingly to accommodate expenses related to his hobbies. Discuss financial priorities and allocate resources as needed to support his interests.

Differing Interests:

Respect and appreciate each other's unique interests. Find a balance between shared activities and individual pursuits to maintain a harmonious relationship.

Encouraging your husband's passions and hobbies is a meaningful way to nurture his personal growth and strengthen your relationship. By actively supporting his interests, you demonstrate your commitment to his happiness and well-being. Remember, fostering an environment where both partners feel supported in pursuing their passions contributes to a thriving and fulfilling marriage. Embrace the opportunity to celebrate his individuality and share in the joy of his achievements, cultivating a bond that grows stronger with each shared interest and new hobby explored together.

Learning and Growing as a Couple

Learning and growing as a couple is a dynamic process that involves mutual exploration, shared experiences, and continuous development of your relationship. Let's look at the importance of learning together, practical strategies for growth, and how to strengthen your bond through shared experiences and ongoing communication.

The Importance of Learning and Growing Together

Building Emotional Connection:

Learning and growing together deepens your emotional bond. Shared experiences create lasting memories and strengthen your sense of partnership.

Enhancing Communication Skills:

Engaging in meaningful discussions and activities promotes effective communication. Learning how to express yourselves and listen attentively strengthens your relationship.

Navigating Challenges:

Growing together equips you with skills to navigate challenges as a team. It fosters resilience and adaptability in facing life's ups and downs.

Shared Goals and Aspirations:

Setting and achieving goals together fosters a sense of unity and purpose. Aligning your aspirations strengthens your commitment and shared vision for the future.

Practical Strategies for Learning and Growing Together

Explore New Interests and Activities:

Try Something New: Experiment with activities neither of you has tried before, such as cooking classes, hiking, or dancing. Exploring new interests together keeps your relationship fresh and exciting.

Cultural Exploration: Attend cultural events, museums, or exhibitions. Learning about different cultures and histories broadens your perspectives and enriches your experiences together.

Read and Discuss Together:

Book Club: Start a book club or read the same book independently. Discussing literature sparks intellectual conversations and encourages mutual understanding of different viewpoints.

Articles and Research: Share interesting articles, podcasts, or research findings with each other. Engaging in intellectual discussions strengthens mental stimulation and deepens your connection.

Attend Workshops and Seminars:

Personal Growth Workshops: Participate in workshops focused on personal development, communication skills, or relationship building. These experiences provide practical tools for growth as a couple.

Relationship Retreats: Attend retreats or seminars specifically designed for couples. These retreats offer opportunities for reflection, communication exercises, and relationship enhancement.

Travel and Explore Together:

Plan Adventures: Plan Adventures: Visit old haunts or travel to new areas. Discovering new places and cultures creates memories that you can share and experiences that deepen your relationship.

Retreats for couples: Think about retreats that blend leisure with activities aimed at personal development. These retreats offer time set aside for introspection, reconnection, and rejuvenation of relationships.

Make and Follow Common Objectives:

Financial Planning: Assist in formulating savings programs and financial objectives. Achieving financial stability for your collaboration enhances trust in resource management.

Health and Wellness: Set fitness goals or dietary changes that you can pursue together. Supporting each other's well-being promotes a healthy lifestyle and enhances your quality of life.

Volunteer and Give Back:

Community Service: Volunteer together for a cause you both care about. Giving back to the community fosters a sense of purpose and reinforces your values as a couple.

Philanthropy: Consider donating to charities or supporting initiatives that align with your shared values. Contributing to causes you believe in strengthens your bond and creates a legacy of compassion.

Benefits of Learning and Growing Together

Increased Relationship Satisfaction:

Engaging in shared learning experiences enhances relationship satisfaction. It promotes mutual respect, appreciation, and a deeper emotional connection.

Improved Conflict Resolution Skills:

Learning how to navigate disagreements and challenges together builds stronger conflict resolution skills. It fosters empathy, compromise, and effective communication.

Sustained Emotional Intimacy:

Learning and growing together nurtures emotional intimacy. It strengthens your connection, creating a supportive environment where you feel understood and valued.

Strengthened Commitment and Partnership:

Pursuing mutual goals and aspirations reinforces your commitment to each other. It deepens your partnership and strengthens your shared vision for the future.

Overcoming Challenges

Differing Interests:

Embrace each other's individual interests and find common ground. Balance activities that cater to both partners' preferences to maintain a harmonious relationship.

Time Constraints:

Prioritize quality time together and schedule activities that fit into your busy schedules. Flexibility and effective time management ensure you make room for shared learning and growth.

Financial Considerations:

Budget wisely and explore affordable or free activities that support your learning and growth as a couple. Focus on experiences that enrich your relationship without straining your finances.

Learning and growing as a couple involves actively engaging in shared experiences, mutual exploration, and continuous development. By prioritizing shared interests, setting mutual goals, and communicating openly, you strengthen your emotional bond and deepen your connection. Together, you and your husband can navigate life's challenges and joys, creating a fulfilling and enduring partnership built on mutual respect, love, and shared learning.

Building a Future Together

Building a future together is a collaborative effort that involves setting shared goals, making plans, and envisioning a life filled with mutual growth and happiness.

Understanding the Importance of Building a Future Together

Shared Vision and Direction:

Planning for the future establishes a shared vision and direction for your relationship. It aligns your aspirations, values, and goals, creating a unified approach to life's journey.

Commitment and Stability:

Building a future together demonstrates commitment and creates a sense of stability. It strengthens your bond and enhances your confidence in navigating challenges as a team.

Long-Term Planning:

Long-term planning ensures you are prepared for life's milestones, such as marriage, children, career advancements, and retirement. It promotes proactive decision-making and financial security.

Personal Growth and Development:

Working towards shared goals encourages personal growth and development. It motivates you to support each other's aspirations and achieve mutual fulfillment.

Practical Strategies for Building a Future Together

Define Your Shared Goals:

Reflect and Discuss: Reflect on your individual aspirations and values. Discuss what matters most to both of you and identify common goals that align with your vision for the future.

SMART Goals: Set SMART (Specific, Measurable, Achievable, Relevant, Time-bound) goals that outline your priorities, such as career milestones, travel plans, family goals, or personal development objectives.

Financial Planning and Management:

Budgeting: Create a budget that accounts for shared expenses, savings goals, and investments. Track your finances regularly to ensure you are on track to achieve your financial objectives.

Saving and Investing: Save for short-term needs, such as emergencies or vacations, and invest in long-term financial security, such as retirement funds or property investments.

Career and Professional Development:

Support Career Goals: Encourage each other's career aspirations and professional development. Discuss career milestones, educational opportunities, and strategies for achieving career satisfaction.

Networking and Mentorship: Build a network of mentors and professional contacts who can offer guidance and support in achieving career goals.

Family Planning and Life Milestones:

Discuss Family Planning: Have open discussions about family planning, including when and how you envision starting a family. Consider factors such as parenting values, childcare arrangements, and lifestyle adjustments.

Celebrate Milestones: Celebrate important milestones together, such as anniversaries, promotions, or achievements. Acknowledge each other's contributions and successes.

Health and Wellness:

Prioritize Health: Make health and wellness a priority for both of you. Establish healthy habits, such as regular exercise, balanced nutrition, and preventive healthcare measures.

Support Each Other: Provide emotional support and encouragement to maintain well-being. Address health concerns proactively and seek professional guidance when needed.

Personal Growth and Relationship Enrichment:

Set Relationship Goals: Define relationship goals that promote emotional intimacy, communication, and mutual support. Regularly assess your relationship dynamics and make adjustments as needed.

Continuous Learning: Engage in activities that foster personal growth and deepen your connection, such as workshops, retreats, or shared hobbies.

Benefits of Building a Future Together

Enhanced Relationship Satisfaction:

Planning and working towards shared goals strengthen your emotional connection and satisfaction in the relationship. It reinforces your commitment and mutual support.

Financial Security and Stability:

Effective financial planning provides peace of mind and ensures you are prepared for future expenses and investments. It minimizes financial stress and promotes financial independence.

Achievement of Mutual Aspirations:

Working towards shared aspirations and milestones brings a sense of fulfillment and accomplishment. Celebrating achievements together reinforces your partnership.

Adaptability and Resilience:

Creating a shared future together fosters resilience and adaptation in the face of adversity. It improves your team's capacity for uncertainty management and problem-solving.

Overcoming Obstacles Differing Objectives:

Find areas of agreement and respect each other's priorities. Align your aims and desires by making compromises and communicating honestly.

Time Restrictions:

Make spending time together to talk and make plans for the future a priority. Set aside time specifically for critical discussions and decision-making.

External Pressures: Remain faithful to your common vision and values in order to manage external pressures, such as familial influences or society expectations. Pay attention to what is most important to you both.

By actively setting goals, encouraging one another's development, and placing a high priority on your mutual well-being, you fortify your bond and provide the groundwork for a happy and long-lasting partnership. Accept the path of creating a future as a team, acknowledging successes, and overcoming obstacles. Together with your spouse, you may build a life full of love, development, and mutual enjoyment via dedication, open communication, and support for one another.

Conclusion

In concluding this journey through the art of romance in marriage, we've explored numerous facets of enriching and deepening your relationship with your husband. From understanding the foundations of love and communication to navigating intimacy, supporting each other through challenges, and building a shared future, each chapter has offered insights and practical strategies to enhance your marital bond.

Romancing your husband isn't merely about grand gestures or fleeting moments of affection; it's a commitment to nurturing a connection that grows stronger with time. It's about celebrating the unique qualities that drew you together and continually investing in each other's happiness and well-being. As you reflect on the principles and practices discussed in this book, consider how they can be tailored to fit your unique relationship dynamics and personal preferences.

Remember, romance manifests in everyday gestures of kindness, in the way you listen attentively, support each other's dreams, and navigate life's challenges hand in hand. It's about creating a space where love flourishes amidst the complexities of daily life, where laughter and understanding are plentiful, and where your bond serves as a source of strength and joy.

As you embark on this journey of romance with your husband, keep these key principles in mind:

Communication is Key: Foster open and honest communication to deepen your emotional connection and resolve conflicts constructively.

Nurture Intimacy: Cultivate physical and emotional intimacy through affectionate gestures, shared experiences, and mutual understanding.

Support and Encouragement: Be each other's cheerleader, supporting dreams and passions, and celebrating achievements, both big and small.

Growth Together: Embrace personal growth and development as individuals and as a couple, exploring new interests and learning from each other along the way.

Build a Future Together: Plan and envision a future that aligns with your shared goals, values, and aspirations, fostering stability and mutual fulfillment.

In essence, romancing your husband is about Fundamentally, wooing your spouse involves valuing the core aspects of your partnership—the giggles, the sobs, the dreams you share, and the intimate moments spent together. It's about enjoying the ride that is marriage and never stopping to rediscover what makes your relationship special and strong.

I hope your marriage regains its passion and delight as you use the lessons from this book in your day-to-day activities. I hope your relationship keeps growing and that it becomes more resilient and loving every day. With the love of your life, here's to a lifetime of romance, connection, and happiness.

Thank you!

Thank you for your purchase. If you enjoyed this book, please kindly consider dropping us a review.